WHAT IS "NATIONAL HONOR"?

THE MACMILLAN COMPANY
NEW YORK · BOSTON · CHICAGO · DALLAS
ATLANTA · SAN FRANCISCO

MACMILLAN & CO., LIMITED
LONDON · BOMBAY · CALCUTTA
MELBOURNE

THE MACMILLAN CO. OF CANADA, LTD.
TORONTO

WHAT IS "NATIONAL HONOR"?

The Challenge of the Reconstruction

BY
LEO PERLA

WITH
A SPECIAL INTRODUCTION BY
NORMAN ANGELL

"What is called NATIONAL HONOR is at present altogether too much a matter of capricious, private, and often merely personal judgment simply because the nations are not as yet self-conscious moral beings."—JOSIAH ROYCE.

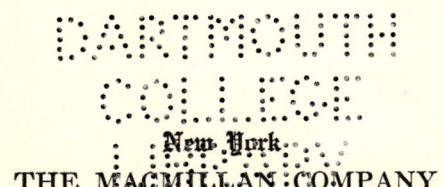

New York
THE MACMILLAN COMPANY
1918

All rights reserved

COPYRIGHT, 1918
BY THE MACMILLAN COMPANY

Set up and printed. Published, April, 1918.

TO
MY WIFE AND COLLABORATOR
REBECCA CUSHMAN PERLA
WHOSE INSPIRATION AND STRENGTH
MADE THIS WORK POSSIBLE

"To argue that a nation's HONOR must be defended by the blood of its citizens, if need be, is quite meaningless, for any nation, though profoundly right in its contention, might be defeated at the hands of a superior force exerted on behalf of an unjust and unrighteous cause. What becomes of national HONOR then?"—NICHOLAS MURRAY BUTLER, President of Columbia University.

INTRODUCTION

It is a hopeful sign that this book which attempts to furnish a reply to the question, "What is National Honor?" should be the work of a young man at the outset of his writing career; that it should be prompted, not by the cynicism of an elderly observer wearied with seeing national honor invoked time after time on behalf of shamefully dishonest causes, but by the sincere desire of a youthful and flexible mind really to know what underlies the potent magic of the word.

It is hopeful, because we have for some years been demonstrating to one another that the old ideals governing national conduct are somewhere defective. Our declared aim in fighting the present war is to destroy certain ideas which have taken possession of the minds of some hundred or more million folk; and if the aggression which those ideas have prompted is dangerous, it is because certain other ideas—including our feeling for "national honor"—which have governed the relations of the western democracies, have stood in the way of a unification sufficient even to enable those democracies promptly to present a common front to a common danger. Had the western world been really unified in our generation, its power would never have been challenged.

If we are to do better in the future, certain fundamental ideas of international relationship must be changed, and change of that character must be the work of minds having the flexibility of youth. It is upon the young men—as many of them as will be left alive—that will fall the task of rebuilding the house which the elder generation has pulled about their ears. If the new is to be sounder than the old the moral foundations will have to be thoroughly and ruthlessly examined.

Perhaps the author of this book will talk to a world a little more disposed to tolerate that probing, than was the world to which some of us talked in that past age which ended in 1914. Perhaps he would say that—he does indeed imply as much in this book—our failure was due in some measure to the fact that we attempted to work through ideas rather than through feelings, that we addressed ourselves to the head, rather than to the heart.

Yet this very criticism of his shows how this discussion of the international problem has shifted in the last fifteen or twenty years. It is almost certain that if he had been writing this book a generation ago, he would have turned his criticism the other way about. This notion of looking upon the internationalist, or peace advocate, mainly as an "intellectual," an over-rationalized person, belongs to the last few years. For a long time previous to that he was looked upon as an over-emotionalized idealist refusing to face with the calm eyes of reason the sordid facts of the physical world, especially certain "biological laws" concerning the struggle for life and the survival of the fit among nations, which a misreading of Darwin has made enormously popular. He was an "amiable and well meaning soul" with his heart in the right place but with a weak head. It is perfectly true that if we go farther back still—to the period of Tennyson's Maude, with its defense of the War fought for the maintenance of Turkish Power, we find an attitude towards the Pacifism of Cobden and Bright not dissimilar to that which now marks the attitude of the man in the streets towards internationalism. As those very practical business men could hardly be represented as dreamers and idealists they were of course sordid bagmen.

We sometimes indeed find the same person revealing this swing between two mutually exclusive appraisements of the motives which push men to war. Even so able and honest a mind as that of the late Admiral Mahan revealed it in striking fashion. In 1908, in his "The Interest of America in International Conditions" he wrote:

"It is as true now as when Washington penned the words, and will always be true, that it is vain to expect nations to act consistently from any motive other than that of interest. That, under the name of Realism, is the frankly avowed motive of German statecraft. It follows from this directly that the study of interests—international interest—is the one basis of sound, provident policy for statesmen. . . . Governments are corporations and corporations have no souls . . . must put first the interests of their own wards . . . their own people."

Yet a year or two later, in criticism of a book of my own, which he conceived to be based on just the assumption of underlying forces in international affairs which he had thus outlined, he wrote as follows:

"The purpose of armaments in the minds of those maintaining them is not primarily an economical advantage in the sense of depriving a neighboring State of its own or fear of such consequences to itself through the deliberate aggression of a rival having that particular end in view. . . . The fundamental proposition of the book is a mistake. Nations are under no illusion as to the unprofitableness of war in itself. . . . The entire conception of the work is itself an illusion, based upon a profound misreading of human action. To regard the world as governed by self-interest only is to live in a non-existent world, an ideal world, a world possessed by an idea much less worthy than those which mankind, to do it bare justice, persistently entertains." [1]

The writer of this introduction has a rather special experience of the changes of attitude just indicated. His first book on international affairs, written on the morrow of the Boer war, and the American conquest of the Philippines, and towards the end of the Dreyfus affair, was an attempt to analyze the nature of patriotism. It leaned strongly to the view that that impulse did not derive its force so much from any rationalized idea of interest as from the desire to satisfy hungry emotions of domination and pride. More constructively, it was a plea for the introduction into national ideals as well as into national conduct, of the standards of private intercourse, where vainglorious pride in power and possessions would send a man to coventry. The book fell entirely flat so far as the public were concerned: had no sale whatever. By the critics it was treated as an interesting example of the extent to which a sentimental idealism could lead a student's gaze away from the real necessities of the hard and work-a-day world in which we live.

[1] *North American Review,* March, 1912.

Fifteen years later the book was followed by a second one, in which an attempt was made to examine critically the assumptions upon which those criticisms had been made. How far could war be regarded as part of the inevitable struggle of men for sustenance? It took very definitely the view that in the last analysis the wars of great modern states were irrelevant to that struggle, that they had no basis in biological necessity or advance, and that their "inevitability" was not rooted in material need or advantage. The author, this time, became for his critics a sordidly minded person who supposed that mankind went to war because it "paid."

My only excuse for recalling this little bit of personal experience is that it does bear rather pertinently on the questions which this book raises: the real springs of human action in such things as international conflict. And human motives are never simple even in individual action. The capacity for self-deception in the interpretation of our own motives even seems illimitable. We may honestly convince ourselves that our motive in a given course is of one kind when it may well be of quite another. The parent who, maddened by the annoyance of a petulant child, finally lets himself go may honestly believe that the terrifying thrashing which he administers is given simply and purely because it is best for the child, "and hurts me much more than it hurts you," when, in fact, it is merely the much needed relief to a long-restrained irritability that has become at last uncontrollable.

Two or three things seem pretty clear in this elusive research. One is that however remote may be the "sense of self-interest," it almost certainly has its place in the feelings which move men in the mass; another is that we are able by a psychological alchemy to transmute the motive of interest into an idealistic one. We can say pretty definitely, for instance, that the institution of domestic slavery had something at least to do with the North and South war; that in a sense the South fought for it and the North against it. Yet it would not do to say that all the idealism was on the side of the North and that the Southerners went to war merely for the profits on slave labor. They fought for their "rights," for their country, the South, for their honor. Yet all those things had formed themselves about an institution that had economic roots, and two rival ideals and systems were in truth involved. On the one side was the slave system which seemed to many Southerners to offer, in a yet undeveloped country, the building up of a civilization that should be stable and secure, promising to the white race on this continent opportunities for an ordered intellectual and political development, a culture touched with refinement and distinction not possible otherwise, and promising to a still savage people a discipline and gradual civilization not possible otherwise. A great deal could be said—and was said—for the idea, though the Southern slave-holders were not perhaps in the best position to be impartial judges of the merits of a system which made of them a privileged aristocracy, the masters of a servile people. Yet genuine loyalties formed about it, and many a gallant gentleman gave his life freely and nobly for an unselfish ideal (after all one cannot well *die* for "profit" unless one is very sure indeed of one's mansion in the next world). But the ideal, however unselfishly supported, was one which, not only had arisen in very definite economic causes, but which millions in the North were giving their lives to destroy believing it to be evil. Here on one side of a line were seven or eight million folk passionately convinced that they had moral right in their favor; and on the other side of the line more millions as passionately convinced that the contrary cause was right. Did the planter's economic relation to slavery play no part in the universal opinion of the South, or was the division of opinion a mere miraculous coincidence? It is no slur upon the memory of very gallant men to say that but for certain economic factors that particular moral conflict would never have arisen.

A generation before the Southern rebellion the British Empire had faced a slavery problem in certain of its possessions. It approached its solution from the economic standpoint and provided for fair compensation for manumission—thanks largely to the efforts of Quakers, who however "sordidly commercial" they might have been were able at least to combine intense feeling on the slavery question with a capacity to see the point of view of the planter. If at that time—during the first half of the nineteenth century—the economic aspect of the Southern problem had been fairly faced by the country as a whole, and the necessity of expending, as an act of economic justice, an amount equivalent say to about one-twentieth of what was finally spent upon the war, the conflict might have been forestalled, the position of the negro in America would be a good deal better than it is; lynching as unknown as it is in Jamaica, and the white race of the South and North alike richer in its original elements, by some millions of Anglo-Saxon stock of the best strain—the children of the men who would have been their fathers if the war had not taken them.

Yet it is the North and South war which is usually cited as the typical instance of the irrelevance of economic issues to the great wars of history.

I had almost written "economic motive"—and should have had to qualify it by saying that the motives were not immediately economic, but were motives arising out of economic issues—and being marvelously changed in the process. For in our psychological analyses we are apt to speak as though a given motive preserved its distinct character when it became associated with others. But the combination with others may absolutely transform it, as certain materials in combination with others undergo wonderful chemical transformations. Nitrogen, in many of its compounds, is a harmless and inert stuff much used by the agriculturist; but this same stuff may become the deadliest explosive known if combined in certain proportions with other equally harmless elements. Nitro-glycerine is a great deal more than the sum of two perfectly harmless materials. The combination has changed the character of both. It would be untrue to say that nitrogen caused the Halifax explosion or that glycerine did; for if either could have been withdrawn, or the two could have been detached and carried separately, there would have been no explosion. To detach the economic element

INTRODUCTION xix

from the sum of those motives which make war, may do a great deal more than merely "take away one of the motives leading to war." It may deprive all the others of their explosive power.

Thus it may be true that German aggression cannot be explained purely in terms of economics, and yet it may be equally true to say that the diversion of the economic motive—a different conception of their interests on the part of the people as a whole—would have neutralized the danger of Teutonic power in the world. And it would be a very bold man indeed who would say that economic motives, ideas as to the material advantage to be derived from the political control of territory, will not play a very large part in the problems of the future—in the destiny of Russia to-morrow perhaps the new sick man of Europe and the spoil of rival imperialisms—in the development of Mitteleuropa, in the relations of Japan to Siberia and China, and those of the United States to Mexico and South America.

To recognize that in the vast economic interests centering around the settlement of some of these territorial problems there are the elements of explosion is not to put forward the proposition that men fight out of a "finely calculated economic hedonism or out of the intellectual persuasion of the advantages of war." It may be perfectly true that the explosion when it comes will be precipitated by some moral question, and yet equally true that if we could have kept the nitrogen of economic interest apart from the glycerine of moral indignation, the explosion would not have occurred.

Despite these reservations, however, I think that Mr. Perla is on the right lines in his insistence upon the need of providing an emotional equivalent for war as the best general method of approach to successful internationalism. Yet the very act of calling attention to the new objective for our emotions, involves an appeal to the intellectual perceptions. It is not so much a matter of appealing to the heart instead of the head, as of appealing to the heart through the head. The heart represents the motive force of our emotions, the head the direction that the force shall take.

I have attempted to illustrate the matter thus: "On the other side of the street you catch a glimpse of a man wanted by the police for the revolting murder of a little girl. At once your sentiment is excited to an intense degree; it blazes up in wild clamor and you give the hue and cry, and the crowd catch the man. And then you seee that on his left hand he has five fingers: the murderer had only two. Now, because your

INTRODUCTION

mind is capable of certain purely logical processes —and thanks only to that—the wild current of your sentiment is immediately changed, and you are now mainly concerned to see that an innocent man does not suffer a threatened lynching. You are just as 'sentimental' as before; the engine of your heart is beating as vigorously, the emotional power is just as great but it happens (to state the thing in mechanical terms) to be turning the wheels of action in an opposite direction because certain levers, which are your mental perceptions, have been shifted by contact with certain facts. A common counsel is: 'The engine alone is what matters; provided only that that has plenty of power you can throw away your steering gear as an encumbrance, and the driver can shut his eyes.' Well, it is because mankind has often been guided by that idea that history is so largely a record of bad accidents.

"For note this: in an age of simpler enthusiasms the steering gear in this case might not have worked so well. In an age when most men believed that any ordinary murderer would not hesitate to call in the ever-convenient witch to remedy so trifling a matter as a missing finger, the simple logical mechanism by which you recognized the man's innocence might not have worked; you would have wanted to see whether God indicated the man's innocence by allowing his arms to be boiled for half an hour without injury. And goodness of heart, the affection of the crowd for their own children, their detestation of so abominable a crime as child murder, would have cost an innocent man his life and fair name."

When the little group of Dreyfusards in the closing years of the 19th Century determined to save France from a militarism which expressed itself in identifying the "honor of the army" with the maintenance of an injustice, and in elevating the irresponsibility of a military court above the honor of justice, they could only in the first instance appeal to intelligence. And if the French had not been an intelligent and an intellectual, as well as an emotional people, the Dreyfusard cause would have been hopeless. Before the Dreyfusards could divert the flow of emotion from one objective—an erroneous and mistaken sentiment of patriotism—to another—the determination that the honor of France should not be rooted in injustice—they had to show first the nature of the thing to which France was committed, and the nature of that to which the revisionists desired her to be committed. The transfer of emotion involved a judgment, a discrimination, comparison, a balancing—an intellectual process. And it is worth noting that "intellectual" as a term of contempt was first used so far as I know by the anti-Dreyfusards who resisted the revision of the Dreyfus trial. Certain it is that that historical re-trial was made inevitable by the work of "intellectuals" who rallied to the defense of Dreyfus. The association between "intellectualism" and Dreyfusism in that affair was unmistakable, and did not escape the notice of the defenders of "the honor of the army." The truth was, of course, that the "intellectuals" were moved by an emotion as intense as that of the military party; but it was an emotion excited by a vision beyond the range of the normal mental eyesight of militarists. It comes down perhaps to this, that as civilization rests in the last resort upon the intelligent coöperation of men for the purposes of fighting the forces of nature, our salvation depends upon discovering with our minds the things that matter, and then giving our emotions free rein. Once having decided with our heads the right course, the more that our hearts can hold us upon it and give our efforts driving force, the better.

But without that intellectual discrimination the choice which is made between two emotional impulses will simply be determined by the relative strength of the two competing emotions—and the strength of an emotional impulse has no relation whatever to its social utility. In society even the instinct of self-preservation is no guide as to its value in self-preservation, as the results of the instinct which prompts five thousand people all to rush for the doors of a building which some one has falsely declared to be on fire, abundantly proves.

Why is it worth emphasizing all this? Because the very proper protest of modern psychologists against the over-intellectualizations of human motive of which their predecessors were guilty, is being used in our time to justify the disparagement of reason, to put forward the dangerous doctrine that judgments which are the outcome of passion are of greater moral worth than those which we reach by emotional discipline and intellectual rectitude. A whole group of interests seem now to be pandering to emotional appetites which can only be satisfied at immense social cost.

It is well to know that so vast a field of our conduct is not rationally motived, that reason plays so small a part therein. The knowledge should be a warning to increase the part of reason, to put us on our guard against unrealized forces that may destroy us as readily as serve us. The glorification of emotion and impulse in politics has come near to wrecking the unity of western democracies and rendering them incapable of that degree of integration which is so necessary if we are to meet such unity and discipline as autocracy manages to impose. Such "instincts" as nationalism, undisciplined and uncontrolled by an intelligent foresight of consequences, are so disruptive a force in any association of states as to make any voluntary unification of our scattered democracies impossible. And if that should prove the case, the last word will be with autocracy, whatever individual military power each one of our nations might achieve. Coöperation between the democracies—which in fact means a democratic internationalism—is the only means by which we can make effective use of our collective power against a common danger. And that coöperation will run counter to many a "natural" impulse.

NORMAN ANGELL.

AUTHOR'S PREFACE

As the molten steel is drawn from the crucible at white heat and poured into forms, so public opinion must be directed in the heat and passion of war, if it is to harden into definite ideals of reconstruction. The purpose of the present work is to aid in the formation of such a public opinion. An untimely discussion of peace may weaken the morale of a country at war; but an inquiry into a technique of reconstruction, when such inquiry is designed to help in the carrying out of the avowed object of the war, can only add strength and purpose to its prosecution.

National Honor has been the cause of almost every war of history. Yet the two Hague Conferences omitted it from their jurisdiction. The League to Enforce Peace disposes of the problem by excluding "non-justiciable" questions (i.e., honor) from the field of its endeavor. Even the Inter-Allied Labor Conference fell a victim to the masked phrase and in its proposal of a court of arbitration to insure the future peace of the world, it excluded all questions of "honor."

National Honor is the fundamental casus belli and the challenge of the reconstruction. To define it is to lay the corner-stone for universal, all-inclusive arbitration without which the peace of the future must rest as a house built upon sands.

My purpose in this work is not to put the question "What is National Honor?" in a spirit of cynicism. In view of the elastic way in which the term has been used to characterize a vague sum-total of national obligations dimly inarticulate, the question is certainly justified. Only when public opinion has become informed of the perversions and misapplications of national honor, will it feel ready to re-christen this popular war-slogan, and to invest it with genuine principles of right and justice.

When the Roman Catholic monk takes the three vows of chastity, poverty and obedience, we know exactly what these ideals are, for which he might be willing to give his life. When a physician speaks of "professional honor," we are no less clear as to the specific, ethical prohibitions that he has in mind. But when a nation declares that "national honor" is the sublime ideal for which it is ever ready to suffer annihilation if necessary, that it is the one thing which it can never consent to arbitrate, we know almost nothing about the implications which the phrase comprises.

If we are to meet adequately the problems of reconstruction, we must resolutely leave behind us the blinding passions and small quibblings of the passing age, and challenge with a ruthless sincerity the values that claim a right to be incorporated into the new and clean fabric which is being put upon the loom.

If the present work succeeds in attracting minds that are capable of considering this problem in the light of international law, and further, if it makes clear the dire necessity for a political analysis of "honor" with the view of arriving at a clearly articulated definition of its more essential imperatives, the object of the author will have been attained. The greatest security of the peace of the world will rest upon a definition and a codification of the principles involved in the evasive phrase which the two Hague Conferences left in sentimental obscurity.

L. P.

New York City.
March 30, 1918.

FOREWORD

I wish to thank sincerely the friends who have helped me in this work. To Frederick P. Keppel, Assistant Secretary of War, I owe a debt which I wish to pay with warm gratitude and affection. His personal interest and effort have been a continued source of encouragement. For Prof. Walter B. Pitkin of Columbia University I feel the obligation which a young writer owes to a recognized journalist for his initial stimulus. I wish to thank Mr. Walter Lippmann for his valuable suggestions to Part III and for his reading of the manuscript. I am indebted to Prof. John Dewey and Prof. Chas. A. Beard for suggestions. Also I want to acknowledge my indebtedness to Mr. Malisoff of Columbia University for sober criticism and to Mr. Yarmolinsky of the College of the City of New York, whose patient criticism and revision of the proofs were invaluable.

CONTENTS

	PAGE
INTRODUCTION BY NORMAN ANGELL	ix
PREFACE BY THE AUTHOR	xxvii
FOREWORD	xxxi

PART I
THE GREAT CONFUSION

I.	PUBLIC OPINION AND HONOR	3
II.	A NEW TECHNIQUE	11
III.	QUESTIONNAIRE—A SYMPOSIUM OF ONE HUNDRED AND THIRTY-FIVE PHASES OF NATIONAL HONOR	30

PART II
A PSYCHOLOGICAL ANALYSIS OF HONOR

IV.	THE EMOTIONAL BASIS OF HONOR	83
V.	TESTING FOR RATIONALITY	99
VI.	TESTING FOR AN EMOTION	112
VII.	DISSECTING THE HONOR COMPLEX	133
VIII.	THE TYRANNY OF A PHRASE	139

CONTENTS

PART III

THREE PROGRAMS FOR PERMANENT PEACE

PAGE

IX. MORALIZATION OF NATIONAL HONOR—A PROBLEM IN ETHICS 151

X. A COURT OF INTERNATIONAL HONOR—A PROBLEM IN POLITICS 165

XI. AN EMOTIONAL EQUIVALENT FOR NATIONAL HONOR—A PROBLEM IN PSYCHOLOGY . . 188

PART I
THE GREAT CONFUSION

WHAT IS "NATIONAL HONOR"?

CHAPTER I

PUBLIC OPINION AND HONOR

As a heritage from the days of dueling the feeling is still current that rational analysis of matters of "honor" is incompatible with "courage." It is undoubtedly a transference of this instinctive belief to the realm of international politics which is responsible for the failure of both Hague Conferences to define the question of "national honor," or even consider it as a proper subject for definition. No better illustration of this universally accepted political dogma can be given than the following citation from Ex-President Roosevelt concerning a possible course of calm deliberation in national disputes of honor.

"It is a preposterous absurdity for a League of nations to attempt to restrain even for a limited time one of its members from declaring war upon another when a question of honor is raised."

In other words it is generally accepted that the

less time that is allowed to elapse between an insult to honor and its vindication, the loftier is the sense of honor. Even though the intervening time may be employed in a sincere effort to ascertain in fairness all possible phases of the dispute, to the ardent champions of this doctrine of haste the delay is nevertheless unjustified.

Added to this instinctive opposition to the use of reason in matters of honor, there has undoubtedly been a conscious evasion of the problem on the part of diplomats. "Diplomacy" has found in the emotional obscurity of honor, political capital. Holls in his work on the "Peace Conference" writes,

"The phrase national honor or vital interests was intentionally made broad and general, and the Conference was well aware that in so doing not only a proper degree of reserve but also possibly a great amount of guilty concealment was being made possible and provided with diplomatic safe-guards."

Public opinion after the war will undoubtedly demand a square and reasonable facing of this apparently elusive problem. If at the time of the Conference (1907) there had existed a public mind alive to its right and obligation to understand this delicate and vital problem, and seeking to form an enlightened judgment as to what the

PUBLIC OPINION AND HONOR

term "national honor" implied, such a complete diplomatic evasion as the Conference was guilty of, would never have been possible.

Were this public blindness to facts less fraught with tragic consequences, one might find in it almost a grim humor. The Hague decided to arbitrate everything "except matters of honor and vital interests." The world heaved a sigh of relief, believing that the possibilities of war had to this degree been removed. However no one whispered to this naïvely credulous world that in so doing the Hague had left still exposed to the wrath of Mars the very things and the only things for which nations have ever fought, and had relegated to the realm of "safe" arbitration, those things for which no nation ever fights. Did a nation ever consciously go to war for something which was incompatible with its "honor"? Do men give their lives for the defense of national dishonor?

The diplomatic manipulation of the term national honor, by which it has been made in diverse ways to cover almost any national policy, has been possible only for the reason that national honor has been accepted by the people of every nation alike as an article of faith. Although its implications are left undefined, no patriot is expected to question the validity of the claim when it is even semi-officially declared to be at stake. The question "What is National Honor?" is therefore a bold and dangerous one to ask. It is true that honor, being an emotional ideal rather than a rational one, is not an easy subject for off-hand definition. As a man of courage is not expected to analyze a point of personal honor, so a self-respecting nation is not expected to descend to the "calculating" plane when its honor is thought to have been wounded.

Fortunately the times seem to give some indication that this melodramatic and irrational attitude is passing. The great war is stimulating a new interest in foreign politics, and diplomatic subtleties. But deeper than this it is purifying and regenerating our sense of values. From the suffering peoples who have been broken on this merciless, gigantic wheel, there will come the ringing question, "What is this national honor which demands our possessions, our happiness, our loves and our lives, and yet which shrinks from arbitration?"

Secret diplomacy on the one hand and woeful public indifference toward the problem on the other, have been the checks upon the development of an enlightened public opinion regarding this most essential factor of international politics. In every emergency, the nature and "constitution" of honor have been left for definition by the people, to diplomats and other "custodians" of the sacrosanct sentiment. The Man in the Street through laziness of thinking and indifference of purpose, shrinks from the responsibility of a decision upon these ethical and political problems. Because of this situation we have developed in our democracies an aristocracy which is the more despotic in its power because of the exclusive quality of the dogmas with which it holds its sway. On occasion of crises, no matter what may be the underlying difficulty in the dispute, it is given to a few dominant personalities to sway the great mass; to mold into a solid body of sentiment, the fragmentary and kaleidoscopic public opinion, by the clarion appeal that the "nation's honor is at stake." Here mob psychology with its geometric progression works with the swiftness of magic.

The few at such critical times are not without an offensive weapon with which to unify the will of the nation. The lash of intolerance forms the back-bone of the attack, followed quickly by that weapon so easily used and so insidious in its effects, the branding-stick which marks the stigma "coward" upon its victim. It is far less difficult for a man to accept the alternative of floating on the tide of public opinion and playing safe, than to hold to a conviction unpopular with a clamorous minority. For this reason the rank and file can be depended upon to fall into line. There is no experience fraught with more expansive complacency than that which comes from basking in the glory of a nation's honor.

There are two possible positions which a man may hold with regard to a dispute of honor in which his nation is involved. He may evince a willingness to die in order to defend what he deems his country's honor to be or he may not recognize that such honor is at stake. If he follow the first course and prove his willingness to die, though later the ideal may prove to be false, he is respected for his sincerity and courage. Should he take the second course he places himself in a position of moral weakness because, although he may manifest a keener understanding and a more sensitive appreciation of ethical subtleties, he has not proved his readiness to die. Although the actual strength and courage needed to defend his position be far greater, it will not save him from the suspicion of his fellows that he is an idealist who believes in safety first "with special reference to his own skin."

The opponent to a proposed war for honor, is placed in the uncomfortable position of feeling

PUBLIC OPINION AND HONOR

that he is a destructive influence, that he is taking away a sentiment for which he substitutes no equivalent, save a rational justification for the repudiation of the sentiment. Even though a majority hold this negative opinion their opposition lacks enthusiasm. If another ideal were supplied in such a case, the crisis might be more easily weathered for the reason that pugnacity once aroused, must have some "ideal" to which to fasten. If robbed of this, albeit by reason, it presents the spectacle suggested in our homely phrase, "a chicken with its head cut off"; a passion of undirected energy.

The remarkable thing has been that in all matters which potentially might be said to involve the honor of nations, in their agreements and foreign policies, men have taken little active interest until friction actually arose and war was imminent. The citizen who allows his country to drift into dishonorable or unjust agreements, or to exercise an ungenerous policy with regard to another country and does not protest in time of peace, can not cancel his obligation as a citizen by bearing arms in defense of his country's "honor" when such a policy has provoked an unjust war.

Since diplomats and statesmen have failed, there devolves upon public opinion the obligation to become interested and enlightened, and the responsibility of imposing order upon the moral confusion into which "national honor" has fallen.

The men who defend this honor must learn to define it.

CHAPTER II

A NEW TECHNIQUE

THE economic case against war has been emphasized so repeatedly in pacifist literature ever since the publication of Mr. Norman Angell's epoch-making work, "The Great Illusion," that one would be justified in assuming that the supreme cause of war has been its supposed promise of economic gain, and that once this theory had been permanently refuted, war will have lost its greatest incentive. President Nicholas Murray Butler of Columbia University puts this universally accepted theory in very effective language.

"We have now reached a point," he says, "where unparalleled enthusiasm having been aroused for a rational and orderly development of civilization through the coöperation of the various nations of the earth, it remains to clinch that enthusiasm and to transform it into established policy by proving to all men that militarism does not pay, and THAT PEACE IS PROFITABLE. JUST SO LONG AS THE GREAT MASS OF MANKIND BELIEVE THAT MILITARY

AND NAVAL RIVALRY BETWEEN CIVILIZED NATIONS CREATES AND PROTECTS TRADE, DEVELOPS AND ASSURES COMMERCE, AND GIVES PRESTIGE AND POWER TO PEOPLES OTHERWISE WEAK, JUST SO LONG WILL THE MASS OF MANKIND BE UNWILLING TO COMPEL THEIR GOVERNMENTS TO RECEDE FROM MILITARISTIC POLICIES WHATEVER MAY BE THEIR VOCAL PROFESSIONS AS TO PEACE AND ARBITRATION AND AS TO GOOD-WILL AND FRIENDSHIP BETWEEN MEN OF DIFFERENT TONGUES AND OF DIFFERENT BLOOD. . . .

"THESE FALLACIOUS BELIEFS ARE NOW THE POINT IN THE WALL OF OPPOSITION TO THE ESTABLISHMENT OF PEACE THROUGH JUSTICE AT WHICH SHARP AND CONCENTRATED ATTACK SHOULD BE DIRECTED. OVERTHROW THESE AND THERE WILL NOT BE MUCH OPPOSITION LEFT WHICH IS NOT ESSENTIALLY EVIL IN INTENT."

This insistence upon the economic incentive as the cause of war carries with it an intimation of a gross libel on human nature. While the economic illusion has undoubtedly held a place in the minds of diplomats and jingoists, in the hearts of the men who fight it has been an irrelevant circumstance. To stress this phase in the hope that a universal acceptance of it will stop war is to work without a recognition of a far more significant factor in human nature, the patriotic imperative. Until the ethical motor-spring in nations

A NEW TECHNIQUE

has been readjusted, there will still be war. In fact the more unprofitable war can be shown to be, the more keenly will men feel the purity of the ideal for which alone they have always been ready to die.

Besides, even with diplomats and statesmen the theory of war's economic stupidity is generally accepted. Who to-day would still defend war from the economic standpoint? It would require a juggling of figures for the militarist to make out a case for war on economic grounds by comparing the staggering sums of money that are being expended in the present world war by either side with the possible cash value of territory or advantage that may come out of the conflict. It may be true that in England before the war there were many who labored under the illusion that if Germany could be eliminated as a commercial rival, any expenditure incurred in achieving it would be a good investment. But three years of war have served a great purpose and have changed public opinion vitally. Whether or not Englishmen have come to accept the truth that the commercial prosperity of Germany or any other country bears no relation to military or political power, no statesman in England to-day would admit that he regarded it as sound national business policy to have expended

$75,000,000,000, the cost of the war to England up-to-date, to cripple German prosperity. If diplomats thought in economic terms before the present war, they think in such terms no longer. Wars to-day are waged on such a tremendous scale and the cost involved is so stupendous that the economic case for conquest and annexation has become absurd and any one who advanced it would lack a sense of humor. War is outrageously unprofitable, even when it results in the acquisition of vast possessions, commercial advantages, concessions, and spheres of influence. If this was true even a hundred years ago how much more true is it to-day when war has assumed such huge proportions that it has become as Bloch prophesied it would become, almost economically impossible to wage it. And since the publication of "The Great Illusion" the notion of the economy of conquest, or the commercial advantage derived from successful war has become obsolete. War is to-day a formidable loss and a stupid business venture.

But though this is generally recognized and accepted it is of no avail in the interests of peace to dwell upon this economic loss and the burdens of debt which the ordeal of battle rolls up. If the recital of the tremendous cost of war has any effect at all upon the common man it is to give him a subtle psychological satisfaction at being associated in the execution of so hugely expensive an enterprise. The very fact that war is uneconomic and almost universally recognized as such, added to the correlative circumstance that men do fight nevertheless, seems to be the greatest and most convincing proof of all that men do not fight for material profit. Human nature would have to have a queer streak in it indeed to persist in an enterprise which it recognizes frankly as unprofitable in the highest degree. The endless array of figures that fill the debit column of the ledger of war are not convincing pacifist argument. They stagger the imagination it is true, but they do not serve as preventives against the recurrence of international conflicts. A man who will cheat his competitor out of a dollar in business, will give up all his substance willingly to serve his country and his convictions. The case is very different from what our economic determinists would have us believe. Men do not fight because of the supposed profit to be derived from war, from a nicely calculated economic hedonism, but in spite of their recognition of its tremendous unprofitableness.

But to say that economic considerations in any phase are not the dynamic force behind war, is not to deny that economic factors enter very seriously into the remoter origins of war. A very important distinction suggests itself at this point. While war undoubtedly has an economic *cause,* it rarely has an economic *motive.* The material of war may grow out of economic conflicts, and rivalries. That is very different, however, from saying that the motive which prompts nations as nations to go to war is a clearly perceived and appreciated desire for economic gain. The difference can be illustrated by an example from every day life. A man might refuse to pay a second fare on a street car and might be willing to argue for an hour with the conductor though his time is worth infinitely more than the maximum gain to be derived from persuading his opponent that he has paid his fare. The dispute unquestionably has an economic cause in that it arose in connection with the payment of fare, but it would be a gross libel on the sense of duty of the conductor and the self-respect of the passenger to accuse either party to the dispute of having an economic motive in continuing it. The analogy will not walk on all fours but it suggests the attitude of nations in going to war. Just as the man's time is worth infinitely more than the possibility of saving his second fare, so a nation's material welfare in every way is much more wisely served by avoid-

A NEW TECHNIQUE 17

ing war. France and Germany nearly came to blows in Morocco over a definite economic matter, the establishment of banks; but if war had not been averted by the Algeciras Conference the motive of Germany would not have been that by going to war she would have been able to control certain banking institutions in Morocco and that such control would have had a greater economic value than the cost incurred in gaining this supposed advantage. Wars are more easily waged when they have a tangible concrete point of departure, but we must not forget that the material consideration involved is the point of *departure* which once it is left must, by the nature of modern war, defeat itself entirely in the carrying out of the spiritual issue which arises from it and which submerges it completely. It is a libel on human nature the unfairness of which has been so repeatedly demonstrated, to recognize material considerations either as an actuating or restraining force toward war. Yet writers to-day would still subscribe to the following words of Lecky,

"Those who will look on the world without illusion will be compelled to admit that the chief guarantees for its peace are to be found much less in moral than in purely selfish motives. The financial embarrassments of the great nations, their profound distrust of one another, the vast cost of modern wars, the gigantic commercial disaster it inevitably entails, the extreme uncertainty of its issue, the utter ruin that may follow defeat, these are the real influences that restrain the tiger passions and the avaricious cravings of mankind."

The economic case for war may in fairness be stated thus; war may have an economic cause; it must have an ethical motive. The war is not conducted however on the plane of the cause but on the plane of the motive. This would be true even if it were not for the fact that men do not fight for material advantage solely. It would be true because the motive and the cause are perceived and adhered to by two clearly defined classes of people within the nation; the motive by those who do the fighting, the cause by those whose interests are involved and appear to be threatened. Consequently the thing which actuates the men in the trenches is not the remoter economic cause with which he has nothing to do, but the immediate motive or occasion, and the reason that he is ready to die, is that he sees in this motive an ethical, spiritual value.

Therefore the pacifist who insists that war can be stopped by removing the economic causes overlooks this infinitely more essential *motive*.

A NEW TECHNIQUE

Since, as we have seen, war can hardly be said to have an economic cause in the sense of an economic motive for gain, it is unjust to credit solely the economic factor with the intrinsic power to make war. A war for any other cause would be equally just and popular provided only it had an ethical motive, and who would say that nations could find no other reason to disagree except on a basis of economic advantage? Religion, nationalism, aggressive ideals, though they have often been used as pretexts for economic gain, were oftener perhaps, the genuine spiritual considerations precipitating conflict.

I believe that the elimination of economic causes if that were possible, would not stop war; it would merely shift the ground, because the root of war is not external considerations or objective ends, but the *moral nature* of men. *Men will fight not so long as they feel it is profitable, but so long as they feel it is right. This impulse to right, regardless of material consequences, is the fundamental cause of war.* Mr. Bertrand Russell puts it thus—

"But war, like all other natural activities, is not so much prompted by the ends which it has in view as by an impulse to the activity itself. Very often men desire an end not on its own account, but because their nature demands the actions which will lead to the end. And so it is in this case; the ends to be achieved by war appear far more important in prospect than they will appear when they are realized, because war itself is a fulfillment of one side of our nature. IF MEN'S ACTIONS SPRANG INDEED FROM DESIRES FOR WHAT WOULD BRING HAPPINESS, THE PURELY RATIONAL ARGUMENTS AGAINST WAR WOULD HAVE LONG AGO PUT AN END TO IT. WHAT MAKES WAR DIFFICULT TO SUPPRESS IS THAT IT SPRINGS FROM AN IMPULSE RATHER THAN FROM A CALCULATION OF THE ADVANTAGES TO BE DERIVED FROM WAR."

Even when a war is clearly a commercial one, it is necessary to give it an ethical appearance if it is to be waged effectively. Mr. Veblen in his recent book, "The Nature of Peace," says;

"These demands (economic) are put forward with a color of demanding something in the way of an equitable opportunity for the commonplace peaceable citizen; but quite plainly they have none but a fanciful bearing on the fortunes of the common man in time of peace, and they have a meaning to the nation only as a fighting unit; apart from the prestige value these things are worth fighting for only as prospective means of fighting. The like appeal to the moral sensibilities may again be made in a call to self-defense, under the rule of live and let live, etc. But in

A NEW TECHNIQUE

one way or another it is necessary to set up the conviction that the PROMPTINGS OF PATRIOTIC AMBITION HAVE THE SANCTION OF MORAL NECESSITY."

Consequently if war is to cease it will be because the moral validity of this ethical impulse has been exploded rather than because its economic futility has been universally accepted. It will be objected here that everybody admits war to be morally wrong. This is not so. If men believed war to be morally wrong it would stop in very short order. Men believe somewhat weakly that it is wrong to kill, to take human life under ORDINARY CONDITIONS. But the men in the trenches to-day certainly believe that there are times when it is morally right to take human life and a good deal of it too. Peace-at-any-price is not a doctrine that attracts very many enthusiasts, while it has a great many more staunch opponents who see in it the lowest depths of immorality. The opposition to peace-at-any-price needs but to be stated to be accepted and yet pacifists labor under the illusion that the moral stupidity of war has been generally accepted. How frequently we hear people lament that though war is admittedly wasteful, horrible, *immoral,* nations will go to war just the same. Such a feeling is fraught with blindness to facts. *Just as nations will go to war in spite of its economic futility so they will go to war only because of its moral validity.* Nations admit that war is horrible and wasteful but they do not admit that it is wrong in the sense that when a nation goes to war for its highest ideals that it is nevertheless immoral. A peace may, according to the majority opinion of writers, be a great deal more immoral than war. The following citation from Mr. James Martineau's speech at the first Hague Conference still voices the conviction of men today.

"The reverence for human life is carried to an immoral idolatry when it is held more sacred than justice and right and when the spectacle of blood becomes more horrible than the sight of desolating tyrannies and triumphant hypocrisies. We have therefore no more doubt that a war may be right than a policeman may be a security for justice, and we object to a fortress as little as to a handcuff."

This identic attitude is expressed by Mr. Roosevelt whose diatribes against an "unrighteous peace" are almost classic. He says:

"Peace is not the end. Righteousness is the end. When the Savior saw the money changers in the temple he broke the peace by driving them out. At that moment peace could have been maintained readily enough by the simple process of keeping quiet in the presence of wrong. Righteousness is the end and peace a means to the end, and sometimes it is not peace but war which is the proper means to achieve the end." ("Fear God and Take Your Own Part," p. 26.)

And the fact that three quarters of the world is at war to-day because of this preference for a righteous war rather than an ignoble peace indicates the weight of the moral argument for war.

Now the generic term for the ethical motives of nations is NATIONAL HONOR. Under this comprehensive term are included all the moral impulses, the spiritual purpose, the motive, the reason, the occasion for war. NATIONAL HONOR is the collective conscience that passes on the justice of all wars, and it is inconceivable that a nation would fight for anything which could not receive the sanction of this moral imperative. "This NATIONAL HONOR is in the nature of an intangible immaterial asset, of course; it is a matter of prestige, a sportsman-like conception, but that fact must not be taken to mean that it is of any the less substantial effect for purposes of a casus belli than the material assets of the community. Quite the contrary, 'who steals my purse steals trash,' etc. In point of fact it will commonly happen that any national grievance must first be converted into terms of this spiritual capital before it is effectually turned to account as a stimulus to warlike enterprise." (Veblen, p. 27.)

Civilized men would not suffer the hell of war for something incompatible with national honor, for something admittedly dishonorable. The point of honor about which war was waged at times may have been spurious, but that is not important or to the point. It is only necessary to concede that patriotically biassed minds sincerely regarded it as a matter of national honor in every case when they went to war. If men sometimes came to fight for points of honor which outsiders did not regard as such, it was because they believed the point to be genuine. The process of this reasoning, of course, is the illogical supposition that because fighting for honor required so much sacrifice, the point of honor therefore is worth fighting for. There is an axiom that nothing which is worth while comes easy which is often reversed to read that everything that comes hard must be worth while. The tremendous sacrifices lend but a glamor to the ideal for which the sacrifices are made and make men fight the harder In short, war without an honor motive as that motive is conceived by each nation is regarded as unthinkable.

From the earliest times we find the ideal of honor as a motive for war and as the irresistible slogan that attracted patriots to give their lives freely in its defense. The ideal of group solidarity and the honor of the group was the pride of primitive man. Even before the nation arose, we had family HONOR, then group HONOR and so on. In Frazer's "Golden Bough" we have mention of HONOR as the elevated ideal of primitive group life.

"The superstitious fear of the magic that may be wrought on a man through the leavings of his food has had the beneficial effect of inducing many savages to destroy refuse. . . . Nor is it only the sanitary condition of the tribe which has benefited by this superstition; curiously enough the same baseless dread, the same false notion of causation has indirectly strengthened the moral bonds of hospitality, HONOR, and good faith among men who entertain it." (Vol. III, p. 120.)

We have HONOR mentioned again and again a little later in the historical development of man, in the Bible. The following from Revelation is one of frequent references to it.

"And the nations shall walk amidst the light thereof; and the kings of the earth bring their glory into it (Holy City); and the gates thereof shall in no wise be shut by day for there shall be no night there; and they shall bring the glory and the HONOR of the NATIONS into it; and there shall in no wise enter into it anything unclean or he that maketh an abomination or a lie" (21-26).

In Greece the ideal of HONOR was sacred and was regarded in much the same way as it is regarded to-day. National HONOR was the noble and elevated motive for entering a war and the thing which consecrated it. In Demosthenes' "Discourse on the Crown" we have the following allusion to this immemorial slogan of war.

"Even though the overthrow may have been a certainty it would be necessary to brave it. There is a thing which Athens has always placed above success and that is HONOR, the elevated feeling of what she owes to her traditions in the past and to her good fame in the future. Formerly at the time of the Persian invasion, Athens sacrificed all to this heroic sentiment of HONOR."

Again and again in every age and period from the dawn of civilized society down to the present day we find continual reference to HONOR as the ideal in every relation of life, for which no sacrifices were too great or unreasonable. It has consecrated wars of every period and as Treitschke has so well said of modern wars—

"Modern wars are not waged for the sake of goods and chattels. What is at stake is the sublime moral good of national HONOR, which has something in the nature of unconditional sanctity, and compels the individual to sacrifice himself for it." ("Politik," p. 128.)

Yet in spite of the fact that this persistent moral impulse of human nature, to which we choose to give the generic term of NATIONAL HONOR, has been the inveterate motive for war, it has nevertheless been given a place of secondary importance in the peace congresses of the past and in pacifist propaganda generally. It has been regarded as so incidental a cause of war that in peace literature we find only casual references to it. At both Hague Conferences the subject of HONOR was not discussed or considered aside from the fact that it was excluded absolutely from the jurisdiction of the proposed Court. When the subject was brought up one diplomat dismissed the problem by saying that "any question may affect the HONOR and vital interests of a nation." And with this vague generality the whole matter was dismissed from even the field of discussion. It is not therefore surprising that in Holl's "Record of the Hague Conference," which is a book of some 590 pages, we have but a single reference to NATIONAL HONOR.

Even contemporary writers mention HONOR as a cause of war in what might be called a "nonchalant" and casual way just as if its significance as the great fundamental "motive" of war were not so absolutely conceded. The significance of it is beginning to be admitted only by the intellectual radicals. National honor as the great irresistible war-slogan is slowly gaining recognition and men are coming to see that the success of the peace movement rests with the enlightened sense of HONOR which will grow out of a bold and fearless consideration of the question at future peace congresses. The following citation from an article on "Patriotism," by Prof. James Harvey Robinson of Columbia University, represents in a beautiful way the beginnings of the new attitude which will be taken toward the question of honor after the present war. It is the more interesting because it contains in spite of its frank recognition of the importance of honor, the cool nonchalance which has so characterized the attitude that is just passing.

"It is *note-worthy* that The Hague Conference did not have the nerve to make questions of national honor matters subject to arbitration. Yet it is just this particular kind of excuse for war which should be most carefully considered before mobilization."

What is this national HONOR which has consecrated almost every war of man and yet which shrinks from arbitration and analysis?

A NEW TECHNIQUE

The consideration of this perplexing problem in the hope of arriving at some adequate answer and solution will be the purpose of the following pages.

CHAPTER III

WHAT IS NATIONAL HONOR? A SYMPOSIUM

CONTAINING ONE HUNDRED AND THIRTY-FIVE CITATIONS ILLUSTRATING DIFFERENT ASPECTS AND VIEWS OF NATIONAL HONOR

ARTICLE nine of the Report of the Second Hague Conference (1907) provided that,—

> "In disputes of an international nature involving neither HONOR nor vital interests and arising from a difference of opinion on points of fact, the contracting powers deem it expedient and desirable that the parties who have not been able to come to an agreement by means of diplomacy should, as far as circumstances allow, institute an international commission of inquiry to facilitate a solution of these disputes by elucidating the facts by means of an impartial and conscientious investigation."

In view of the very serious limitation which this clause imposes upon the jurisdiction of the Hague it is very important to know more accurately what an exemption of disputes of "HONOR" properly includes. The vital questions which suggest themselves in this connection are: "What is national honor?" "Is there any consensus of opinion as to what it implies?" It is clear that at the end of the present war, the statesmen and the people generally of the belligerent countries will make a serious attempt to lift the whole question of national honor out of its emotional obscurity in an effort to define it upon universal and generally accepted principles of right and justice. It is therefore opportune for us to attempt to clear our own minds on the question of honor in order to attain to a thoroughly rational and definite idea of its implications. For the purpose of arousing discussion which may serve as a basis for the consideration of the question at the Peace Congress which will meet at the close of the present war, this symposium has been prepared.

DO THE QUESTIONS RAISED BY THE FOLLOWING CITATIONS, IN YOUR OPINION, INVOLVE "NATIONAL HONOR"?

NATIONAL PRIDE

Punctilios of Honor, National Self-Assertion, National Courage, and Expiation for offenses to national honor.

1. Insult to the flag by an official representative of a foreign power.

"Any one who even superficially attacks the Honor of a state, challenges by his action the very nature of the state.— If the flag of the state is insulted it is the duty of the state to demand satisfaction and if satisfaction is not forthcoming to declare war however trivial the occasion may appear."—Treitschke, "Politik," p. 125.

2. Disregard of the conventional punctilios governing diplomatic intercourse.

"This National Honor is subject to injury in divers ways, and so may yield a fruitful grievance even apart from offenses against the person or property of the nation's business men; as for example through the neglect or disregard of the conventional punctilios governing diplomatic intercourse, or by disrespect or contumelious speech touching the flag, or the persons of national officials, or again by failure to observe the ritual prescribed for parading the national honor on stated occasions."—Thorstein Veblen, "The Nature of Peace," p. 29.

3. Maintaining relative political prestige.

"National Honor for the nation which is considering it at the time, consists for her that she should maintain herself just as she is in her rank and place in the hierarchy of nations."—Terraillon, "L'Honneur," p. 255.

4. Resisting the demands of another country to be "consulted in any further exploitation of the globe."

Typical case: England disallowed Germany's claim in this connection at the time of the Moroccan dispute.

A SYMPOSIUM

"The claim that Germany made, that no treaty should be made in any part of the world without the approval of Germany, was not one which a *self-respecting* nation could admit."—Professor Gilbert Murray, cited in Bertrand Russell, "Justice in Wartime."

And at the same time—

5. Demanding this privilege "for one's own country" to be consulted in all treaties henceforth to be made.

    Typical case: England demands to be consulted in all treaties concerning Morocco.

"But if a situation were forced upon us in which peace could only be preserved by the surrender of the great and beneficent position which Great Britain has won by centuries of heroism and achievement, by allowing England to be treated where her interests were concerned as if she were of no account in the cabinet of nations, then I say emphatically that peace at that price would be a HUMILIATION INTOLERABLE FOR A GREAT POWER LIKE OURS TO ENDURE."—Lloyd George, Mansion House Speech, July 21, 1911.

6. Demanding to be consulted in any "further exploitation of the globe."

    Typical case: Germany demands to be consulted in the Moroccan treaty.

"Germany has risen to a world power and our Honor demands that we be consulted in any further exploitation of the globe.— When we fell out with France in the

Moroccan dispute, we had our NATIONAL HONOR to defend."—VON BULOW, "Imperial Germany," p. 96.

7. Demanding to be consulted in any and all treaties made by other powers.
    Typical case: Germany in the Moroccan dispute.

"Our HONOR demands that no treaty should be made in any part of the world henceforth without the approval of Germany."—Kaiser's Speeches.

8. Resisting the command of another power to settle an international question in a certain way.
    Typical case: President Cleveland compelled England to submit the Venezuelan Boundary dispute to arbitration.

"Was not the NATIONAL HONOR of Great Britain at stake when Lord Salisbury as representative of the great British Empire was told by President Cleveland that he must arbitrate a controversy? I do not believe the government of Great Britain had heard talk of that kind since the Battle of Waterloo."—FRED. COUDERT, before the Washington Association of New Jersey, Feb. 22, 1912.

9. Being compelled by threat from another power to modify a political ambition to extend a country's influence by royal intrigues.
    Typical case: Germany desired to place a Hohenzollern on the Spanish throne

1867; France made Germany withdraw the candidature.

"This impression of a wound to our sense of NATIONAL HONOR so dominated me that I had already decided to announce my retirement."—BISMARCK, "Gedanken und Errinerungen," p. 94.

10. To show national courage as a virtue in itself regardless of the justice or right of the provocation that may arouse it;

"Nevertheless we have seen that when nations renowned of old for their valor have been freed from all danger, when they have been forbidden the use of arms, when they have lost that standard of HONOR which makes them brave death, we have seen them lose the very strength which sustains the domestic virtues."—SISMONDI, quoted by Novicow in "War and Its Alleged Benefits," p. 7.

11. To demand indemnity for violations suffered at the hands of another power.

>   Typical case: An English freighter, the *Alabama* manned in British waters, was allowed to escape and prey upon American ships. We demanded indemnity for the loss suffered.

"No case in modern times has afforded a better pretext for the avoidance of submission to arbitration than the *Alabama* case. Here if ever it might be maintained that the HONOR of the two nations was concerned. Great Britain was charged with evading the rules of just international intercourse by allowing the *Alabama* to escape and prey upon our commerce.— This was an imputation which might well throw the British Chauvinist into a delirium of patriotic indignation.— The United States might well on its side have regarded this as an insult to its NATIONAL HONOR."—COUDERT, "Anglo-American Treaty," p. 52.

12. To refuse the payment of indemnity claims. Typical case: England in the *Alabama* controversy.

"We will not lose sight of the fact that even in the pecuniary claims, in almost every case a nation may refuse arbitration on the pretense that the very advancement of such claims is a reflection upon its HONOR."—HON. JACKSON RALSTON, "Disputes and Arbitration," p. 2.

13. To oppose arbitration for the payment of an indemnity.

"That (*Alabama* claims) is a question of HONOR which we will never arbitrate for England's Honor can never be made the subject for arbitration."—LORD JOHN RUSSELL.

14. Retreating from a position taken in a dispute.
Typical case: President McKinley in the Cuban Controversy.

"President McKinley said: 'In the name of humanity, in the name of civilization, in behalf of endangered American interests which gives us the right to speak and to act, the war in Cuba must stop.' The American people thus stood committed to a most serious business—we had taken a position (war), from which we cannot retreat in HONOR, to be maintained if through peace no less resolutely than through war."—"Conscience of the Nation," Sermon on the Liberation of Cuba by WILLIAM JEWETT TUCKER, 1898, College Church Opening.

15. Fighting to a finish after being reluctantly drawn in.

"I assume that there is no one at the present time so ignorant of the spirit of the American people that he would not be willing to admit the truth of the following proposition—that if our country is drawn into any war although against our will and against our desire we will nevertheless fight to the finish for our NATIONAL HONOR and integrity."—PRES. HIBBEN, "Higher Patriotism," p. 25.

16. To continue in a war although later evidence shows cause of war to have been unjustly conceived.

"Whatever good reason there may have been for recognizing that our (English) claims of sovereignty in the Transvaal rested on a mistaken view of native sentiment, and however fairly such recognition might have been allowed to affect the ultimate settlement, the game of war once entered upon ought to have been played out until it was either lost or won. To this the HONOR of the country was fully pledged."—H. I. D. RYDER in *Nineteenth Century*, referring to Boer War, 1899.

17. To recede from a position unjustly taken.

"HONOR does not forbid a nation to acknowledge that it

is wrong, or to recede from a step which it has taken through wrong motives or mistaken reasons."—ADMIRAL MAHAN, "Moral Aspect of War," p. 32.

18. Refusal to render apology for offense.

"There will never be a case in which NATIONAL HONOR is more dangerously and vitally affected than it was in the Dogger Bank incident. The danger lay in the fact that the HONOR of the Russian fleet was in question when Lord Lansdowne demanded apology, compensation, and the punishment of the offending officers."—L. S. WOLFF, "International Government," p. 49.

19. Do public lies or verbal threats wound HONOR?

"In your letter you say that your enemies by their lies and calumnies are endeavoring to stain the HONOR of Germany in her hard struggle for existence."—S. W. CHURCH, to Doctor Shafer. Open Letter.

20. Do Honor wounds come from without, or within?

"In what one of our ordinary differences with Great Britain has our Honor become so delicately involved that the delicacy of its constitution required a prompt and vigorous régime of blood and iron. And yet we have had hot and long disputes when honor might have been called to the front by either nation and made the pretense for a refusal to arbitrate. A nation's honor I would venture to say is never compromised by temperance nor injured by forbearance. A nation's honor is not served by rash counsels nor by violent impulses recklessly indulged in. It is indeed a frail and delicate possession if it cannot live in an atmosphere of peace; it is a dangerous one if it is tarnished by friendly discussion and a disposition to hearken to the voice of justice. National honor may perhaps shine all the brighter when a great nation is slow to admit that her just dignity may be imperilled by the act of others. THE HONOR OF A NATION IS IN HER KEEPING NOT IN THAT OF HER NEIGHBORS: IT CANNOT BE LOST SAVE BY HER OWN ACT."—COUDERT, *ibid.*, p. 37.

21. Same as 20.

"Our country cannot be dishonored by any other country or by all the powers combined. It is impossible. ALL HONOR WOUNDS ARE SELF-INFLICTED. We alone can dishonor ourselves or our country."—ANDREW CARNEGIE.

22. Must National Honor have "pecuniary vindication"?

"It is true that where the point of grievance out of which a question of the NATIONAL HONOR arises is a pecuniary discrepancy, the national honor cannot be satisfied without a pecuniary accounting."—VEBLEN, "Nature of Peace," p. 29.

23. Can Honor wounds be Healed by "words"?

"When duly violated the NATIONAL HONOR may be made whole again by similarly immaterial instrumentalities; as e.g., by recital of an appropriate formula of words, by formal consumption of a stated quantity of ammunition in the way of a "salute"; by "dipping" an ensign and the like procedure which can of course have none but a magical efficacy."—VEBLEN, *ibid.*, p. 29.

INTERNATIONAL POLITICS

Imperialism, "Spheres of Influence," National Aggrandizement, Boundaries, Protection of Citizens, Sovereignty.

24. To build up a great Empire reluctantly.

"Britain like Rome before her built up her Empire piecemeal; for the most part reluctantly, always reckoning up the cost, labor and burden of it; hating the responsibility of *expansion,* and shouldering it only when there seemed to be no other course open to her in HONOR and safety."—F. S. OLIVER, "Ordeal of Battle."

25. To keep in subjection people of a lower civilization.

"When you talk of conquest you mean England in Egypt, yes, you do, and you refuse to see that we have to hold high the HONOR of our country and to protect our dominions in the East."—HALL CAINE, "White Prophet," p. 62.

26. To conquer other people out of a recognition of the law of "survival."

"Success in the struggle for survival is followed by the second degree of militancy, that of *conquest,* in which militancy becomes a positive instead of a negative factor. It is in this metamorphosis, out of the red chrysalis that the race rises upward on the pinions of an eagle.— Commercialism grows as militancy deteriorates since it is in itself a form of strife but without HONOR or heroism."—GENERAL HOMER LEA, U. S. A., "Valor of Ignorance," p. 45.

27. To seize and dominate alien country.
Typical case: Germany invades Belgium.

"We will remain in the Belgian Netherlands to which we will add the narrow strips of coast as far as Calais.— After having vindicated our HONOR we will return to the joys of work and only take up the sword again if you try to force from our grasp what our blood has won for us."— MAXIMILIAN HARDIN, in a résumé, *London Daily Chronicle*.

28. To expand at the expense of neighboring country for the sake of power, or prestige.
Typical case: Frederick the Great desired to expand into a great power.

"It has become essential to enlarge the territory of the state and corriger la figure de la Prusse, if Prussia wished to be independent and to bear with HONOR the great name of Kingdom."—TREITSCHKE, "Deutsche Geshichte," V. 1, p. 51.

29. To maintain a sphere of influence in an unexploited territory unhampered.
Typical case: France in Morocco.

"He (M. Delcassé) declared that France could not go to the proposed international Conference (i.e., Algeciras that was to be), without DISHONORING herself."—Paris Correspondent to the London *Times*, Oct. 9, 1905.

30. For another growing power to try to force an entrance into such a "sphere of influence."

Typical case: Germany in Morocco.

"When we fell out with France in the Moroccan question, we had weighty interests of our own and our NATIONAL HONOR to defend."—VON BULOW, "Imperial Germany," p. 56.

31. To resist the cession of one country to another of an adjoining strip of territory which might destroy the "balance of power."

Typical case: Prince of Orange in 1866 wished to cede Luxemburg to Napoleon.

"We must show our confidence in the energetic Prussian policy by our unflinching firmness.— We will not seek to avoid war when we are in danger of being wronged. If we allow this (cession of Luxemburg to France) to pass in silence and without opposition—how indelible a blot will stain the HONOR of Germany."—HERR VON BENNIGSEN, Leader of the National Liberals in the Reichstag, April 1, 1866.

32. To maintain supremacy in any part of the globe.

Typical case: Japan in the East.

"An attempt to disallow the Japanese claim to predominance in the Eastern part of Asia, and to the domination of the Asiatic Seas, would violate their conception of NATIONAL HONOR."—VON BERNHARDI, "Britain as Germany's Vassal," p. 124.

33. To insist upon a boundary line.

Typical case: "54–40 or fight."

"Irritating questions have undoubtedly arisen and the war-like element has sometimes asserted itself, as when it declared it was a question between 54–40 or fight; but our practical good sense overcame the ultra-patriotic men who were burning to immolate themselves on the altar of the country's Honor."—Fred. Coudert, "Anglo-American Arbitration Treaty," p. 51.

34. To hold foreign territory the ownership of which is in dispute.
> Typical case: The boundary dispute between Italy and Switzerland over the district of Peschiaro.

"For many years there had been a dispute between Switzerland and Italy on a question of boundary respecting the frontier near Peschiaro. It was just one of the questions that formerly would have led to war for it has been held among nations as a scrupulous point of Honor not to surrender one inch of territory except at the edge of the sword."—Mr. Henry Richard at the Peace Conference at Cologne, 1881.

35. Forcible dispossession of other nations.

"With some gift for casuistry one may at least conceivably hold that the felt need of Imperial self-aggrandizement may become so urgent as to justify or at least to condone forcible dispossession of weaker nationalities. This might, indeed it has, become a sufficiently perplexing question of casuistry both as touches the punctilios of National Honor and as regards an equitable division be-

36. The question of citizenship.

"This tribunal would lay down the rule that the territorial integrity of each nation was inviolate, that it was to be guaranteed absolutely its sovereign rights in certain particulars including for instance the right to decide the terms on which immigrants should be admitted to its borders for purposes of residence, citizenship or business; in short all its rights in matters affecting its HONOR."—THEODORE ROOSEVELT, "America and the World War," p. 237.

37. The protection of citizens residing or sojourning in foreign country.

"Solidarity is also in a uniform and permanent manner an integral part of NATIONAL HONOR. No state permits another to oppress her subjects, to outrage them, to treat them in a fashion which would not conform to international conventions, the rights of man or to human dignity. What would be in truth a nation which would not be able or above all would not wish any longer to protect her subjects."—TERRAILLON, "L'Honneur," p. 262.

38. To oppose "Capitulations."

"It is an awakening of NATIONAL HONOR which has affected in regenerated Turkey a public movement for the suppression of "capitulations" which allows Christian governments to exercise over their subjects in Turkey their exclusive jurisdiction, through their middle men, their ambassadors and consuls."—TERRAILLON, "L'Honneur," p. 261.

39. The question of political independence or sovereignty.

"There is a national HONOR which is fixed and permanent.— Every nation claims at first its political independence."—TERRAILLON, "L'Honneur," p. 260.

40. Discrimination against citizens residing in a foreign country.
Typical case: In 1913 California passed legislation prohibiting Japanese from holding land in that state.

"How long are we to bear the disgrace and humiliation which seems to grow worse every year.— How can we expect our countrymen to be respected in America when our foreign office does not even strive to uphold our NATIONAL HONOR?"—Editorial in *Osaki Mainichi*, May 3, 1913.

41. The matter of National Culture and sovereignty.

"German majesty and HONOR falls not with the Prince's crown;
When amid the flames of war, German Empire crashes down.
German greatness stands unscathed."—SCHILLER, 1797.

INTERNATIONAL LAW

Treaties, Alliances, Neutral Rights, International Guarantees.

42. To hold a treaty when economically unprofitable.
> Typical case: Congress revoked the discriminating clause against British shipping in the Panama Canal controversy.

"We certainly are not at liberty to discriminate against British ships using the Panama Canal because it is a violation of the rule of equality which we have solemnly accepted and adopted, asserted and reasserted, and to which we are bound by every consideration of HONOR and good faith."—ELIHU ROOT, *Independent,* Feb. 6, 1913.

43. To break a treaty when economically unprofitable to keep it.

"A state recovers more easily from material losses than from attacks upon its HONOR. . . . When a state realizes that existing treaties no longer express the actual relations between the powers, then if it cannot bring the other state to acquiesce by friendly negotiations, the only other course is to declare war."—TREITSCHKE, "Politik," p. 546.

44. To keep and break the same treaty.

"They (pacifists) have advocated the silly and wicked peace commission treaties which have actually been adopted by our government during recent years; treaties which in any serious crisis this nation would certainly break; treaties which it would be DISHONORABLE to break, and far more DISHONORABLE in any crisis to keep."—THEO. ROOSEVELT, *Metropolitan,* February, 1917.

45. To respect treaties of alliance.
   Typical case: Japan's alliance with England in the present war.

"Every sense of loyalty and HONOR oblige Japan to coöperate with Great Britain to clear from these waters the enemies who in the past, present and future menace her best interests and her people's lives."—Japanese Premier on Japan's entrance into the war.

46. To break treaties of alliance.
   Typical case: Italy and the Central powers in the present war.

"Blessed are the young men who hunger and thirst after HONOR for their desire shall be fulfilled."—D'ANNUNZIO writing about Italy's entrance into present war.

47. To respect international guarantees.
   Typical case: England entering the war in defense of Belgium because she was a signatory to the treaty which guaranteed Belgian neutrality.

"If I am asked what we are fighting for I reply in two sentences. In the first place to fulfill a solemn international obligation which if it had been entered into between private persons in the ordinary concerns of life would have been regarded not only as an obligation of law, but of HONOR which no self-respecting man could have repudiated."—Hon. H. H. Asquith in House of Commons, Aug. 6, 1914.

48. To break any provisions of international law.

"The Honor of no country can be concerned in breaking the terms of a treaty or recognized principles of international law."—Lowes Dickenson, "Foundations of a League of Peace," p. 10.

49. To oppose privateering.

"When the *Alabama,* fitted in a British port, swept our commerce from the ocean, was not our National Honor at stake?"—Coudert, *ibid.*

50. To seize ships because of a difference of opinion as to the rights of those ships to fish in certain waters.

Typical case: British ships were seized in Bering Sea.

"We seized British ships in the Bering Sea and condemned them in our ports, a most grievous insult according to the sensitive and self-constituted custodians of British Honor; but Great Britain adopted peaceful counsels and a wise court heard, examined and decided the case without any apparent injury to British Honor."—Coudert, *ibid.*, p. 40.

51. The swaying of a nation from neutral position.

"Even among a people with so single an eye to the main chance as the American community it will be found true on experiment or on review of the historical evidence, that an offense against the NATIONAL HONOR commands a profounder and more unreserved resentment than any infraction of the rights of persons or property simply. This has latterly been well shown in connection with the maneuvers of the several European belligerents designed to bend American neutrality to the service of one side or another. Both parties have aimed to intimidate or cajole."—VEBLEN, "Nature of Peace," p. 28.

52. To maintain neutrality according to international convention.

"Nations like Switzerland or Belgium would make it a point of HONOR to guard inviolate the neutrality granted them by treaties."—TERRAILLON, "L'Honneur," p. 256.

53. Rights of neutral ships in time of war.

"But surely the Dogger Bank's Fisheries case was a question of HONOR.— The action of Admiral Rozhdestiensky in firing on the trawlers, sinking the Crane, wounding six fishermen and killing two, was described as an unspeakable and unparalleled and cruel outrage."—GOLDSMITH, "League to Enforce Peace," p. 100.

54. To insist on an exclusive right to fish in certain seas.

"When in 1891 Canadian vessels engaged in seal hunting were seized in Bering Sea by our revenue cutters there was talk of NATIONAL HONOR on both sides of the ocean.— COUDERT, *ibid*.

55. To reject judicial investigation for the determination of points of fact.

Typical case: There was question as to

>   whether the assassins of the late Archduke of Austria were Serbs or not, but Austria refused to accept judicial procedure.

"The question for example of the alleged duplicity of the Servian government in the Serajevo assassination affecting as it undoubtedly did both HONOR and vital interests was eminently suitable for arbitral decision."—J. HOBHOUSE, "Toward International Government," p. 37.

56. The interpretation of contracts or treaties.

"The board (International Insurance) according to the scheme proposed a minimum of judicial powers. These judicial powers would never refer to questions which could be called questions of national HONOR. The judicial problems of the board would be limited to questions referring to the actual interpretation of certain contracts."—JOSIAH ROYCE, "War and International Insurance."

57. The breaking of pledges.

"It is admitted by all honest men that the German government has from the violation of the neutrality of Belgium all through the war repeatedly broken her solemn pledges, resorted to every trick, device, falsehood and dishonest method to gain her ends, sacrificing the last remaining shreds of NATIONAL HONOR and culminating her national shame by deliberately breaking her promise to this country."—FREDERICK BOYD STEVENSON, "Showing Up the Shame of Socialism," Brooklyn *Daily Eagle,* June 10, 1917.

58. Carrying out obligations with revolutionary government that were concluded with pre-revolutionary government.

Typical case: England's treaties with Czar and the Revolution in Russia.

"Treaties concluded with Russia before the Revolution were still binding," Lord Robert Cecil explained in the House. "Until the new Russian government released the allies Great Britain was bound in HONOR to carry out her engagements."—LORD ROBERT CECIL, in Commons, May 16, 1917. New York *Tribune* report.

INTERNAL POLICY

Revolution, Sedition, Strengthening Political Faction, Carrying out domestic policy.

59. To resist any interference from without with a domestic policy.
    Typical case: British authorities in 1841 permitted the *Creole* to go free though it carried a slave cargo.

"Bitter indeed was the feeling and loud the clamor of those who look upon force as the vindicator of HONOR when the British authorities at Nassau in 1841 permitted the slave cargo of the famous ship *Creole* to go free.— The case was submitted to arbitration, a judgment rendering adequate compensation to the owners of the vessels was obtained and the United States without cost or treasure found its contention vindicated and its NATIONAL HONOR satisfied."—COUDERT before Washington Association of New Jersey, Feb. 22, 1912.

60. To keep out emigrants.

"The two treaties submitted remove the exceptions made in their predecessors as to questions affecting NATIONAL HONOR and substitute a statement of the scope of arbitration which is designed by its terms to exclude all questions not properly arbitrable.— One of the first of sovereign rights is the power to determine who shall come into the country and under what conditions."—Report of Com. on Foreign Affairs, U. S. Senate, Aug. 15, 1911.

61. To carry out or strengthen a domestic policy.
Typical case: Bismarck desired the unification of Germany and felt that a war with France would consummate it.

"Our national sense of HONOR compelled us in my opinion to go to war and if we did not act in accordance with the demands of that feeling we should lose when on the way to its completion the entire impetus toward our national development won in 1866."—BISMARCK, "Gedanken und Errinerungen," p. 140.

62. For a section of a country to demand independence.
Typical case: The South asked for independence in 1860.

"In our judgment the Republicans are resolute in their purpose to grant nothing that will or ought to satisfy the South; we are satisfied the HONOR, safety and independence of the Southern people require the organization of a Southern Confederacy."—"Southern Manifesto," Dec. 14, 1860.

63. For a country about to be disintegrated to resist such demands.

> Typical case: The North in the Civil War.

"That to the Union of the States this nation owes its unprecedented increase in population, its HONOR abroad and the "Platform of NATIONAL HONOR" by Nicolay and Hay: union as denying the vital principles of a free government and as an avowal of contemptible treason which it is the imperative duty of an indignant people to rebuke and forever to silence, etc."—From the Platform of the Republican National Convention, May 16, 1860, characterized as the "Platform of NATIONAL HONOR" by Nicolay and Hay: "Lincoln." Complete Works.

64. Cases 62 and 63 together.

> Typical case: Norway and Sweden separate in 1905.

"Who does not remember the waves of nationalism that swept the country in 1905. . . . One spoke in Sweden then just as one speaks in the warring countries now of NATIONAL HONOR, national safety and national existence."—ELLEN KEY, "War, Peace and the Future," p. 11.

65. To disregard the wills of subjects in the matter of governing them after they have been torn away from their mother country as a result of a victorious war.

> Typical case: Germany seized Alsace in 1870 and governed them against their will.

"The world will recognize that in disregarding the will of the Alsatians of to-day we are only fulfilling an injunction imposed by our NATIONAL HONOR."—TREITSCHKE, "Politik," p. 56.

66. Removing an undesirable official.

"If the great inert mass of German descent has any conscience will it accept the barbarous doctrines of Mr. Morgan's partner without uniting in a protest to the President and declare its refusal to contribute to the Red Cross until this person has been removed from the dominant position he holds in its Councils? Or will it silently acquiesce and suffer this stain on American Humanity to defile our NATIONAL HONOR?"—Editorial, "Issues and Events," June 30, 1917.

67. Pacifist agitation within a country not yet at war.

"The agitation of the League to Enforce Peace at this time" (after Belgium was invaded but before we declared war) "is therefore a move against international morality, against our own NATIONAL HONOR and vital interests and in the interests of international immorality."—THEO. ROOSEVELT, *Metropolitan*, February, 1917.

68. To show united front in time of war to foreign country.

"It is to be hoped that President Wilson in his Conferences with Mr. Dent and the other recalcitrant members of the committee has not spared the rod. For the President must appreciate more keenly than any other American that the United States cannot afford to create the appearance

even of a desire to mark time till the allies win the war. To leave an opening for such a charge against this country would be to deal American PRESTIGE a blow from which it could never recover. The dark influences in Congress which have BESMIRCHED OUR GOOD NAME among the nations already must not be permitted to add this crowning SHAME."
—Editorial, *Evening Sun,* April 10, 1917.

69. To subscribe to war loans.

"We urge upon every reader of the New York *Times* the necessity of immediate investment in the Liberty Loan. The subscriptions must close next Friday.— It would be a DISHONOR in which the whole nation would share if the total amount were not subscribed for by June 15."—New York *Times,* June 11, 1917.

70. As a cause of sedition.

"It is equally easy to discover the effect of HONOR and the sense in which it is a cause of sedition. Sedition is produced by the sense of DISHONOR done to ourselves and by the sight of the HONOR enjoyed by others. But the case is one of injustice when neither the HONOR or DISHONOR is disproportionate, and of justice when it is proportionate to the merit of the persons concerned."—ARISTOTLE, "Politics," p. 345.

71. Universal military service.

"In many long years of bitter servitude God taught our people to look to itself, and under the pressure of the foot of a proud conqueror our people engendered in itself that most sublime thought that it is the highest HONOR to dedicate one's blood and purse to the Fatherland in her armed

"IDEAL SELF PRESERVATION"

Vengeance, Retaliation, Protection, Defense, Regaining Lost Provinces.

72. To retaliate in a subsequent war for defeat suffered at the hands of an enemy.

"If we beat Germany and then humiliate her, she will never rest until she has redeemed her HONOR by humiliating us more cruelly in turn."—ARNOLD TOYNBEE, "Nationality and the War," p. 4.

73. Vengeance.

"Among the tribes, the cities or the hostile states as among hostile families, vengeance was always an obligation of HONOR; in the same way each member was, as formerly in the family, responsible for the actions of another member or of those of the social groups in its entirety."—TERRAILLON, "L'Honneur," p. 254.

74. To try to regain territory lost through an unsuccessful war.
   Typical case: Alsace and Lorraine lost by France in 1870.

"The return of Alsace and Lorraine to France is the first demand of our NATIONAL HONOR."—VIVIANI on his American Mission.

75. Same as 74.

Typical case: Italy and Trentino.

"Blessed are the young men who hunger and thirst after HONOR for their desires shall be fulfilled."—D'ANNUNZIO writing about the nationalist spirit in Italy (Irredenta movement).

76. Same as 74. As applied to territory never owned but merely conquered.

Typical case: England and the reconquest of the Sudan.

"In fact there was never a moment that the thought of the eventual reconquest of the Sudan and of the retrieving of the HONOR of British arms was not before them" (British).—H. A. GIBBONS, "New Map of Africa," p. 2.

77. Revenge.

"What now is NATIONAL HONOR? It is not Honor to be hunting for imaginary insults. It is not Honor to look on one's neighbors with suspicion. Revenge is not HONOR."— REV. CHAS. DOLE, "Democracy."

78. Readiness to fight.

"It is not HONOR worthy of civilized men to be quick to take up arms and to fight."—REV. DOLE, *ibid*.

79. Immediate resentment and unwillingness to delay.

"It is a preposterous absurdity for a league of nations

to attempt to restrain even for a limited time one of its members from declaring war upon another when a question of Honor is raised."—Theodore Roosevelt, Letter, New York *Times,* Jan. 21, 1917.

80. Protection and defense against attack.

"The vital interests of Austria-Hungary were at stake and she had to protect herself. . . . Threatened in her vital interests Austria-Hungary chose the way which Honor and duty prescribed."—From the Austrian Red Book.

81. To wage defensive but never offensive war.

"If this struggle was forced upon Germany then indeed she stands in a position of mighty dignity and Honor and the whole world should acclaim her and succor her.— But if this outrageous war was not forced upon her would it not follow in the course of reason that her position is without dignity or Honor."—S. Warden Church, President Carnegie Institute of Pittsburgh, in an open letter Nov. 9, 1914.

82. To strike back when attacked or rights are invaded.
Typical case: Germany invaded American rights on the Seas by her submarine warfare.

"I have said nothing of the governments allied with the Imperial government of Germany because they have not made war upon us and challenged us to defend our rights and our Honor."—Pres. Wilson, Declaration of War, April 2, 1917.

83. Maintenance of territorial integrity against invasion.

"The only effective way to free Germany from such fear (aggression from without) is to have outside nations like the United States in good faith undertake the obligation to defend Germany's HONOR and territorial integrity if attacked, exactly as they would defend the HONOR and territorial integrity of Belgium or of France if attacked."—THEO. ROOSEVELT, "America and the World War," p. 234.

84. Defense.

"What has war ever done to settle great questions?— I speak not of defensive wars—but of war as a conflict between two independent nations striving to obtain satisfaction for wounded HONOR, or to settle a boundary question, or to collect a financial claim."—FRED. COUDERT, "International Arbitration," p. 27.

85. Defense.

"We entered the war, at least that is my understanding, to protect our own rights, to defend and make secure the lives of our people, and to maintain our own dignity and HONOR and prestige among the nations of the earth. Why not say so? It is not only the truth, but it is infinitely more important that it be said than that we undertake to carry on the war upon the strength of vague and ever receding generalities."—SENATOR BORAH, New York *Times*, Sunday, June 3, 1917.

86. Defense and protection.

Typical case: Germany declares war on Russia.

"In pursuance of her historic traditions Russia, sister in blood and creed of the Slav nations, has never remained indifferent to their fate." (The document then points out that Austria's bombardment of Belgrade led the Russian government to issue orders that the army and the navy should be mobilized, that Germany demanded the revocation of these measures and, upon the refusal, suddenly declared war upon Russia.) The manifesto then continues: "It is no longer a question of taking the part of a sister nation unjustly wronged, but of defending the HONOR, dignity and integrity of Russia and her position among the great powers."—From War Manifesto issued by the Czar on July 20, 1914.

MORAL PRINCIPLES

Spreading Civilizations, Missions, Humanity, Justice, Democracy, Honesty

87. To lend material and moral aid to nations fighting for "principle."

Typical case: France helped America in Revolution.

"France's NATIONAL HONOR has always consisted in lending material and moral aid to those who fight for a principle or an ideal and to awaken in the consciences of those outside of her frontiers ideas of justice and liberty."
—TERRAILLON, "L'Honneur," p. 260.

88. To protect helpless nations against massacre.

England aided Armenia against Turkish oppression repeatedly.

"It is in the name of NATIONAL HONOR that England has always protested against the inhuman acts or the useless cruelties—against the Armenian massacres."—TERRAILLON, "L'Honneur," p. 259.

89. To oppose slavery.

"It is in the name of national HONOR that England has placed her diplomatic and naval forces in the service of anti-slavery."—TERRAILLON, "L'Honneur," p. 257.

90. To propagate ideas of civilization.

"England has always considered as an integral part of her national HONOR to propagate over the whole world ideas of civilization and progress."—TERRAILLON, "L'Honneur," p. 257.

91. "Missions" of civilization.

"National HONOR according to the nation which is considering it at the time consists for her in conserving with her traditional qualities her particular institutions and the MISSION which she has or believes she must fulfill."—TERRAILLON, "L'Honneur," p. 256.

92. "Progress toward human freedom."

"Any man who touches our HONOR is our enemy. Any man who stands in the way of that kind of progress which makes for human freedom cannot call himself our friend."—WILSON, May 16, 1917.

93. To establish democracy in a foreign country.

"Let us without one hour's delay put the American flag on the battle-front in this great war for democracy and civilization.— We owe this to humanity—most of all we owe it to ourselves, to our NATIONAL HONOR and self-respect."—THEO. ROOSEVELT, asking Congress for Volunteer Army, April, 1917.

94. To spread a type of civilization by force of arms.

"We must grow into a world power and stamp a great part of humanity with the impress of the German spirit. If we persist—in the dissipation of energy—there is imminent fear that in the great contest of the nations we shall be DISHONORABLY beaten."—BERNHARDI, "Germany and the Next War," p. 114.

95. To liberate a neighboring people which is being oppressed by a foreign power.
> Typical case: Cuba unjustly governed by Spain aroused America to go to war for its liberation in 1899.

"We both felt very strongly that such a war (against Spain) would be as righteous as it would be advantageous to the HONOR and interests of the nation."—ROOSEVELT, referring to himself and Gen. Wood, "Roughriders," p. 5.

96. To help the "weak."

"Our flag for HONOR ever stands
　To lift the weak, to lead the free.

America our blessed land is calling, calling thee."
—Mrs. Halsted, in a poem presented to War Department.

97. Honesty.

"The phrase Honor and vital interests embodied the conscience of states. Honor or its cognate honesty speaks for itself; neither man nor nation should consent to that which is before God a shame to do or to allow."—Admiral Mahan, "Armaments and Arbitration," p. xvii.

98. Case 97.

"What attitude should politics take toward falsehood? We reply that political activity is connected with a public office, obtained by inheritance or appointment, but no office or relation of service can authorize or compel the commission of dishonorable and morally unlawful acts." —Rumelin, "Relation of Politics to Moral Law," p. 69.

99. To espouse the cause of small nationalities. Typical case: Uruguay breaks with Germany for the defense of Belgium.

"President Viera in his message to the Parliament declared that the Uruguayan government had not received any direct offense from Germany but that it was necessary to espouse the cause of the defenders of justice, democracy, and small nationalities."—Lead to this article in New York *Times,* Oct. 7, 1917, was "Uruguay breaks with Germany on ground of Honor."

100. Internationalism.

"We are anti-patriot internationalists and have in no degree a love for the mother country. Hence we do not know what NATIONAL HONOR is. . . . It is a matter of indifference to us whether we are French or German. As for the defense of our mother country we will give neither one drop of blood nor one square centimeter of skin."—M. GUSTAVE HERVE, quoted by Sir Arthur Conway in "Crowds in War and Peace," p. 279.

101. A question of morality.

"What is called NATIONAL HONOR is at present altogether too much a matter of capricious, private, and often merely personal judgment simply because the nations are not as yet self-conscious moral beings."—JOSIAH ROYCE, "War and Insurance," p. xxiv.

102. The double standard.

"Thus we may meet the old assertion that the laws of private honor do not apply to national affairs. They apply whenever men care to apply them."—STRATTON, "Double Standard."

PERSONAL AS RELATED TO NATIONAL HONOR

103. Transferring personal into national honor.

"It was so at Syracuse in the olden days when a political revolution was the consequence of a quarrel between two youths of official rank about a love affair. In the absence of one of them one of his companions seduced the object of his affections, and the aggrieved person in his indignation against the offender retaliated by inducing his wife to commit adultery. The result was that they gradually collected adherence among the members of the governing class until they had arrayed the whole body in two opposing factions."—ARISTOTLE, "Politics," p. 351.

104. Insults by "Representative Men."

"Must we then consider the possibility of war with England over some fancied insult or question of NATIONAL HONOR? It is certain that representative men of both nations have no slightest disposition to insult or prejudice or injure the people of the other nation."—REV. CHARLES DOLE, "Spirit of Democracy."

105. Personal Wrongs.

"At Mitylene it was a feud arising about heiresses that proved to be the beginning of a world of troubles and more especially of the war with the Athenians in which their city was captured by Paches. The circumstances were as follows: A rich citizen named Timpphanes died, leaving two daughters. Dexandros, who had been a rejected suitor for them on behalf of his sons, became the prime mover in the feud and as he was Athenian counsel at Mitylene incited the Athenians to declare war. Again in Phocis it was a quarrel of which an heiress was the subject between Mnasias, the father of Mneson, and Euthycrates, the father of Onomanchus, that proved to be the beginning of the Phocian SACRED war. And lastly the polity of Epidamaus was revolutionized in consequence of a marriage engagement. A person who had secretly betrothed his daughter to a young citizen being fined by the father of his future son-in-law in his official capacity felt the INDIGNITY so acutely that he formed an alliance with the unenfranchised classes in the state to effect a revolution."—ARISTOTLE, "Politics," p. 352.

66   WHAT IS "NATIONAL HONOR"?

106. Personal Insult to National Prestige.
Typical case: Senator Kellogg accuses Senator LaFollette of making false statements with regard to America's entrance into the war.

"I am as jealous of the right of free speech as any member of this body, but this is a question of erroneous statement of facts rather than of free speech. I have no right to wish to criticise any man who voted against this nation going to war although I may disagree with him; but we are at war, and I believe men of this body, men of influence, should not make statements tending to aid and encourage the enemy, and to cast DISHONOR and discredit upon this nation."—SENATOR KELLOGG in the Senate, Oct. 7, 1917.

107. Individual pledging the honor of the country without the consent of the legislative body.

"The Foreign Secretary pledged our HONOR to defend France in certain contingencies behind the back of Parliament and the Nation."—G. LOWES DICKINSON, referring to Entente Cordiale in "The League of Peace," p. 12.

108. Similarity between personal and national honor.

"And the lesson which the shock of being taken by surprise in a matter so deeply vital to all the nations in the world, has made poignantly clear is, that the peace of the world must henceforth depend upon a new and more wholesome diplomacy. . . . It is clear that nations in the future must be governed by the same high code of HONOR that we demand of individuals."—PRES. WILSON in "The League to Enforce Peace," May 26, 1916.

109. A "dead sailor" and NATIONAL HONOR.

"Even a dead sailor or a live artist may affect a nation's HONOR or conceivably even its vital interests."—L. S. WOLFF, "International Government," p. 52.

ECONOMIC MATTERS

110. To collect the debt owing by citizens of one country to citizens of another.

"It can scarcely be alleged that anything like an international consensus now obtains as to the ethical propriety of forcing a nation to pay its creditors. The principle at stake though novel and important can hardly be said to touch vital interests or NATIONAL HONOR."—ADMIRAL MAHAN, "Practical Aspects of War," p. 61.

111. To force a nation to open its ports to commerce.
Typical case: England forces China to open its ports in 1861 to British commerce.

"It is in the name of HONOR that England once believed it possible to force China to open her doors to the commerce and the ideas of the West."—TERRAILLON, "L'Honneur," p. 260.

112. Difference of opinion with regard to the use of national insurance funds.

"Differences of opinion concerning the use of the insurance fund would frequently involve what is usually called NATIONAL HONOR. They would therefore be hopeless differences."—JOSIAH ROYCE, "War and Insurance," p. xix.

113. Foreigners and the ownership of land. Typical case: Japanese land-holding in California.

"It seems then that there is a sort of honor which does not allow a stranger to establish himself in a region as a landed proprietor."—TERRAILLON, "L'Honneur," p. 252.

114. The question of the loss or depreciation of business interests.

"In case it should happen that these business interests of the nation's businessmen interested in trade or investment abroad are jeopardized by a disturbance of any kind in these foreign parts in which their business interests lie, then it immediately becomes the urgent concern of the national authorities to use all means at hand for maintaining the gainful traffic of these businessmen undiminished, and the common man pays the cause. Should such an untoward situation go such sinister lengths as to involve actual loss to these business interests or otherwise give rise to a tangible grievance it becomes an affair of the NATIONAL HONOR, whereupon no sense of proportion as between the material gains at stake and the cost of remedy or retaliation need longer be observed, since the NATIONAL HONOR is beyond price."—THORSTEIN VEBLEN, "The Nature of Peace," p. 27.

115. The definiteness of HONOR as a moral ideal.

"A large proportion of the questions embraced under HONOR and vital interests are precisely in that inchoate condition of non-decision and even of dispute which cannot be brought under the head of law. . . . All efforts fail because we are dealing with men's consciences, their honor and vital interests."—ADMIRAL MAHAN, *ibid.*

116. Interests and HONOR as synonyms.

"Within fifteen years Japan has twice found it essential to go to war on account of interests in Korea; interests by her esteemed so vital to her people and their future that she could not with HONOR submit the decision of them to any judgment but their own."—ADMIRAL MAHAN, "Neglected Aspects of War," p. xvi.

UTILITY OF HONOR

117. As an aid to the creation of a nation:

"The Italian national HONOR existed before modern Italy; it is the idea of national HONOR which made her."— TERRAILLON, "L'Honneur," p. 252.

118. Its use for a material purpose.

"National HONOR is a highly valued asset or at least a valued possession; but it is of a metaphysical, not of a physical nature, and it is not known to serve any material or otherwise useful end apart from affording a practicable grievance consequent upon its infraction."—VEBLEN, *ibid.*, p. 29.

119. Its economic value.

"This national HONOR, which so is rated a necessary of

life is an immaterial substance in a peculiarly high-wrought degree, being not only not physically tangible, but also not even capable of adequate statement in pecuniary terms, as would be the case with ordinary material assets."—VEBLEN, *ibid.*, p. 29.

DEFINITION

120. Honor as an evolution.

"But HONOR, as the term is applied, is a mental concept varying with the mood of the times."—RALSTON, *ibid.*, p. 5.

121. Distinction between disputes of HONOR and other disputes.

"One must repeat that to make arbitration obligatory is impossible if you try to distinguish questions which do and do not affect HONOR and vital interests. The distinction is based neither upon reason or fact."—L. S. WOLFF, "International Government," p. 52.

122. Any question as a possible HONOR dispute.

"It is amusing to read after days and days of discussion that one diplomatist at length remarked that any question may affect the HONOR and vital interests of a nation."—L. S. WOLFF, *ibid.*, p. 51.

123. HONOR as a peculiar possession of each nation.

"And one may even show that each nation has a particular concept and a more or less clear idea of what HONOR means to it."—TERRAILLON, "L'Honneur," p. 215.

124. Same as 123.

"I know but one thing; it is that we again have a German Empire, a German Emperor and a German HONOR."—SUDERMAN; "Le Conjure Socrate."

TRADITION; PAST AND FUTURE OF A NATION

125. The perpetuation of a national culture.

"It is a nice question whether in practical effect the aspiration to perpetuate the national culture is consistently to be distinguished from the vindication of the national HONOR."—VEBLEN, "The Nature of Peace," p. 23.

126. Loyalty to hatred and friendships.

"HONOR to a nation is then the claiming of loyalty to herself, to her friendships, to her justified hatreds and her legitimate aspirations."—TERRAILLON, "L'Honneur," p. 261.

127. The obligation a nation owes to her past and to her future.

"Even though the overthrow may have been a certainty it would be necessary to brave it. There is a thing which Athens has always placed above success, and that is HONOR, the elevated feeling of what she owes to her traditions in the past, and to her good fame in the future. Formerly, at the time of the Persian invasion, Athens sacrificed all to this heroic sentiment of HONOR."—DEMOSTHENES, "Discourse on the Crown."

128. The respect for tradition.

"The Government of the living by the dead which we have shown as an essential part of family HONOR, we find it again at the foundation of NATIONAL HONOR. Not only in ancient cities, but even in modern states."—TERRAILLON, "L'Honneur," p. 251.

MILITARY HONOR

129. Divisions of military HONOR.

"No. 1. Escape of interned prisoners.
"2. Sponsions.
"3. Tacit agreements.
"4. The abuse of the White Flag.
"5. Ruses or stratagems.
"6. Spies.
"7. Treachery and criminal warfare."—STOWELL and MUNRO, "International Cases," Vol. 2, Table of Contents.

130. Balance of military force.

"And so, in presenting them to you, who at this tragic hour judge the destinies of the belligerent nation, we indulge a gratifying hope that they (suggested peace terms) will be accepted, and that we shall thus see an early termination of the terrible struggle which has more and more the appearance of a useless massacre.

"Everybody acknowledges, on the other hand, that on both sides, the HONOR of arms is safe. Do not then turn a deaf ear to our prayer, accept the international invitation which we extend to you in the name of the Divine Redeemer, the Prince of Peace."—The Pope's Appeal to the Rulers of the Belligerent Peoples, given at the Vatican, Aug. 1, 1917.

POSITIVE OR CONSTRUCTIVE SIDE OF HONOR

131. The relative importance of the debit side of Honor.

"To preserve her Honor should be the nation's main purpose and object, but she should not readily believe those who tell her that by hard blows alone may its integrity be protected. A nation's Honor consists in her fidelity to her engagements, in carrying out her contract in spirit as well as in letter, in paying her just debts, in respecting the rights of others, in promoting the welfare of her people, in the encouragement of truth, in teaching obedience to the law, in cultivating honorable peace with the world."— Frederic Coudert, *ibid*.

132. Honor at stake in time of peace.

"Is a nation's Honor at stake only in times of imminent peril? I crave for every one of you a like spirit of consecration for the tasks of peace."—Pres. Grier Hibben, Sermon at Princeton University, June 13, 1915, "Martial Valor in Time of Peace."

133. Constructive aspect.

"Must we then consider the possibility of war with England over some fancied insult or question of National Honor? It is certain that the representative men of both have not the slightest disposition to insult, to prejudice, or injure the people of the other nation. There has been immense gain in this respect on both sides in fifty years. What now is national Honor? It is not Honor to be hunting for imaginary insults, it is not Honor to look on one's neighbors with suspicions, it is not Honor worthy of civilized men to be quick to take up arms and to fight. Revenge is not Honor. Is it not national Honor to be humane and friendly?"—Rev. Charles Dole, "Spirit of Democracy."

HONOR AND PEACE

134. To give up plans of conquest and the maintenance of honorable peace.

> Typical case: Germany gradually gives up her plans of conquest without feeling a depreciation of her national Honor.

"It is interesting to note that Bethmann-Hollweg did not feel himself strong enough at this time to declare himself openly a partisan of the Annexationist plan. We may gather from this that there is a strong demand in Germany for peace with Honor, but not with conquest. This is a hopeful sign."—Editorial, New York *Tribune*, May 17, 1917.

135. Honorable peace and the emancipation of enthralled population.

"If the war is to end in an honorable peace there must be annexation, continuing the emancipation of the enthralled population who are laboring under despotism, and the retention of strategic positions as safeguards against future attack."—Ex-Premier Asquith, in House of Commons, May 17, 1917.

HONOR AND PUBLIC OPINION

136. Honor and public opinion.

"I hear much about the Honor of our country, and I believe the Honor of this country should be maintained, but I want to see the term Honor defined by the men who have to maintain it. I would not like to have some fat fellow define my Honor, tell me when it had been assailed, and shove me into a fight."—Hon. Denver S. Church, in a speech in the House of Representatives, April 26, 1916.

NATIONAL HONOR AND ARBITRATION

"Might it not be felt that the Honor and vital interests of a nation are better conserved by accepting a reward impartially decided by the merits of the case than by insisting on the ordeal of battle?"—J. Hobhouse, "Towards International Government," p. 40.

"Great Britain and the United States pledged themselves to abide by that tribunal (Geneva) whatever it might be. That decision in due time was rendered; and the two nations do abide by it. Did it ever enter the thought of the British nation to refuse obedience to that decision because it was in some sense adverse to her? To her eternal Honor be it said no."—At the Hague, "An International Tribunal," Dr. James P. Miles, 1875.

"In no case that I can recall has a great nation dishonored her hand and seal by refusing to carry out the decrees of the tribunal to which she has submitted her claims and her arguments."—FREDERIC COUDERT, "Annual American Arbitration Treaty," p. 53.

WILLINGNESS TO ARBITRATE

PRESIDENT NICHOLAS MURRAY BUTLER

"To argue that a nation's HONOR must be defended by the blood of its citizens, if need be, is quite meaningless, for any nation, though profoundly right in its contention, might be defeated at the hands of a superior force exerted on behalf of an unjust and unrighteous cause. What becomes of national HONOR then?"

EX-PRESIDENT WILLIAM HOWARD TAFT

"If now we can negotiate and put through a positive agreement with some great nation to abide the judication of an international arbitral court in every issue which cannot be settled by negotiation, no matter what it involves, whether HONOR, territory or money, we shall have made a long step forward by demonstrating that it is possible for two nations at least to establish as between them the same system of due process of law that exists between individuals under a government."—Before American Society for Judicial Settlement of International Disputes, December, 1910.

EX-PRESIDENT WILLIAM HOWARD TAFT

"Personally I do not see any more reason why matters of NATIONAL HONOR should not be referred to a Court of Arbitration than matters of property or matters of national proprietorship. I know that it is going further than most men are willing to go; but I do not see why questions of HONOR may not be submitted to a tribunal, supposed to be composed of men of HONOR, who understand questions of national Honor, and then abide by their decisions as well as any other question of difference arising between nations."—March, 1910. Address, Amer. Peace and Arb. League.

ALFRED H. FRIED

"Moreover people are apparently ignorant of the fact that new and powerful factors have appeared with an interest in the prevention of war, and that in many cases, conflicts, even those involving Honor and vital matters, can at the present time, be settled in a manner consonant with reason and worthy of humanity."—"German Emperor and Peace of World," p. 185.

COSMOS

"For example, if the international commissions of inquiry are to be really valuable, the limitations imposed upon it as to disputes of an international nature, that involve either Honor or essential interests must be removed. It is a poor sort of international dispute in which some one cannot find a point involving either Honor or an essential interest. "The Basis of Durable Peace."

FRED. COUDERT

"If our National Honor were concerned, it is gravely alleged, no aspersion on that delicate organ could be treated otherwise than with bombs and guns. A great nation cannot talk when her Honor is assailed; action must then be prompt and energetic."—*Ibid.*, p. 50.

FRED. COUDERT

"National Honor is a sonorous phrase under which the civilized man cloaks those feelings of the primitive man only partially submerged within him. The emptier and vainer a nation's intellect, the greater becomes the clamor for national Honor. We talk of national Honor. How many questions of national Honor have we not submitted to a court? Has not almost every arbitration that the United States has had with Great Britain been based upon a controversy which might have been tortured into a question of NATIONAL HONOR and which a lot of jingoes said were questions of national Honor and hence opposed it?"—Washington Ass. of N. J., Feb. 12, 1912.

HERR DERNBERG

" 'Questions of HONOR and national self-preservation can never be submitted to Courts of Arbitration.' I take the liberty of differing with him. Every officer whose HONOR is insulted is not permitted to take up arms without further ado; he must submit to a court of HONOR composed of his friends, and these are in duty bound to try every means in their power to bring about an honorable compromise. Nations too must do that."—In New York *Times*.

CARL SCHURZ

"Does not this magnificent achievement (*Alabama* claims) form one of the most glorious pages of the common history of England and America. Truly the two great nations that accomplished this need not be afraid of unadjustable questions of HONOR in the future."

MRS. MEAD

"Justice and HONOR are larger words than peace, and if fighting would enable us to get justice and maintain Honor, I would fight, but it is not that way."

L. S. WOLFF

"The past has shown that nations can and will accept judicial decisions in questions affecting HONOR and vital interests provided that (1) a rational and suitable judicial procedure exists, and (2) the question can be put to the Tribunal in a logical form."—"International Government," p. 48.

A SYMPOSIUM

FRED. COUDERT

"Above all let us not be misled by high sounding phrase about national Honor. The only danger which our Honor may run is an exaggerated tendency to make readiness to strike the test of its delicacy and the proof of its existence."—*Ibid.*, p. 59.

FRED. COUDERT

"Tradition has ordained that a nation's Honor had to be lubricated with blood in order to be kept in good working condition. Both of the conflicting nations usually assured the other nations that were looking on of the imperative necessity under which the honor of the other was placed to do some fighting to make it fresh and bright. When a sufficient number of men had been slaughtered, and a proper number of towns had been burnt and plundered, and when the treasury of either or both was empty, Honor smiled once more with restored cheerfulness, made her graceful obeisance and retired from the scene leaving the victor to have his way. Honor, National Honor, has been a priceless possession but a very expensive one to keep, the more expensive because of its uncertain character, its vague definition and its unreasonable demands. . . . The salutary process of a blood baptism can alone renovate and preserve this delicate and susceptible quality of a nation's Constitution."—*Ibid.*, p. 46.

UNWILLINGNESS TO ARBITRATE

VON BERNHARDI

"Even if a comprehensive international code were drawn up no nation would sacrifice its own conception of right to it. By so doing it would renounce its highest ideals; it would allow its own sense of justice to be violated by an injustice and so dishonor itself."—"Germany and the Next War," p. 32.

Do Arbitration Treaties compromise the Nation's Honor by their very nature?

VON BERNHARDI

"Arbitration treaties must be peculiarly detrimental to an aspiring people which has not yet reached its political and national zenith and is bent on expanding its power in order to play its part HONORABLY in the civilized world."—"Germany and the Next War."

PART II

A PSYCHOLOGICAL ANALYSIS OF HONOR

CHAPTER IV

THE EMOTIONAL BASIS OF HONOR

THE foregoing pages if they do not prove that national honor as an ethical ideal is an empty phrase, at least suggest its elastic quality. When a phrase can be used to condone so many varied and even contradictory aspects of national conduct, so many cases of questionable sincerity, and so many obvious injustices, it is not unfair to question its rational character. It is clear from an analysis of the symposium that national honor as it is conceived by representative statesmen, is a chaotic notion, that far from being a definite ideal it is an all-embracing moral caption, and that in acquiring the wealth of its implications, it has lost its moral significance.

Those who delight in reducing all human action to a nicely calculated economic hedonism will explain this confusion into which the ideal of honor has fallen, by the fact that diplomats have persistently misapplied the term with conscious hypocrisy. Such an accusation is unfair and unpsychologic. Whatever the evils of secret diplomacy it could never have gone the extreme of unscrupulous deception in the name of national honor. While there may be instances in history of Machiavellianism where a diplomat consciously misused and misapplied the slogan of national honor in order to rouse a patriotic fervor among his compatriots for an unjust war, it is hardly possible to account for this confusion by the wholesale indictment that diplomats have desecrated the ideal of honor by malicious intent. If the average man, as it is said, is a good deal below the average in other respects, he is a good deal above the average when his country's honor is in any way involved and when he uses the word in justification for certain actions. National honor is a collective, social ideal, and it is well-known that in the face of collective aims or ideals even the meanest men rise above the petty motives which might influence them in ordinary life. On the level of the herd instinct men are as equally capable of the most altruistic conduct as they are incapable of calculated unscrupulousness.

The charge of hypocrisy besides being unfair is inadequate as an explanation for the confused state in which we find the notion of honor. Psychologists repeatedly warn us against the "intellectualist" fallacy, the notion that human conduct is the result of an intellectual process in

THE EMOTIONAL BASIS OF HONOR

which the end, and the means to the end, are coolly and deliberately calculated before hand. The charge of hypocrisy is an undeserved tribute to the rational character of human nature, while it does not do justice to the great emotional wellsprings and impulses that account for our actions in nine out of ten cases. The fair explanation for the mental gymnastics which the ideal has been made to perform is that without taint of insincerity and without any conscious encouragement, it has become a beautiful delusion—beautiful because the adherence to it even as a delusion affords a very positive joy and calls forth some of the most beautiful qualities of human nature.

That it is unfair and foolish to attempt reform by inviting antagonism and ill feeling, needs no lengthy exposition in these days of reform penology. Criminals are no longer reformed by being continually reminded that they are the most wicked and hopeless that have ever been. Even if there were not a shadow of a doubt that diplomacy has been as corrupt as the above hypothesis would suggest, it would be bad psychology to approach the subject of political reform in the spirit of such a recognition.

We can analyze out without difficulty the elements that account for the delusion. Honor like all moral ideals is a growth, and in the process of its evolution four variable factors were concerned. The abstraction of honor, never having been defined in an even approximate way or clearly conceived, could not accurately have been handed down from one generation to the next. Each generation received a set of traditional notions about honor and unconsciously modified them so that the succeeding generation inherited somewhat different traditions. While the new accretions to the ideal may have been dimly perceived by the generation contributing them, the inherited accretions were much more dimly conceived, if at all, in the shadowy region of emotional association. And so if the generation contributing the new variations of national honor apprehended them in only the most general way, it is easy to understand why a great confusion presents itself now after dozens of generations have lived and died and fastened their emotional and intellectual associations to the ideal. We might call this the subjective variable in the complex. Then there is an objective variable that is equally complex. National institutions, war, and political machinery in connection with which national honor arises, have also been changing, and consequently modifications and influences were at work on the ideal from the outside.

Between the two, national honor has lost most of its rational quality, but has retained in a cumulative way, emotional power and manifold associations.

There are two other variable factors which have entered into the mental processes by which the term has lost its specific quality. Not only has the ideal of national honor changed from generation to generation in the natural course of evolution, but it has at no time even in the same generation had anything like a universal interpretation. Just as each nation feels it has a peculiar mission in the world, a mission that is necessarily colored and determined by its history, its traditions, its political institutions, its culture and its aspirations, so every nation has its own peculiar ideal of honor which is a direct development and outgrowth of these distinctly national peculiarities. Each nation believes sincerely that its honor is a peculiar possession of its political constitution and must necessarily be different from the honor of its neighbors. Universality is the last thing in the world to expect of the ideal of honor. The reason for this is not hard to find. For example we can readily see that the Monroe Doctrine is a peculiar policy of honor which has grown out of the historical development of the United States, and that it would be illogical for Japan or Russia, let us say, to claim the Monroe Doctrine as a matter which its honor includes and which it must defend at all costs.

The vigorous opposition to the arbitration of honor disputes arises from a frank recognition of the peculiarly national character of it, and the impossibility of universalizing it as a guiding principle for arbitration. That no foreigner can render a "just decision" in matters affecting "the vital interests of honor" of another country, is an opinion which we have heard only too often from opponents of all-inclusive arbitration agreements. Mr. Roosevelt recognizes the local quality of honor when he says—

"This proposal (Mr. Roosevelt's) therefore meets the well-founded objections against the foolish and mischievous all-inclusive arbitration treaties recently negotiated by Mr. Bryan, under the direction of Pres. Wilson. These treaties— explicitly include as arbitrable—questions of honor and vital national interest."

We have this same silent recognition of the peculiar quality of honor by Von Bernhardi. He says in this connection—

"Even if a comprehensive international code were drawn up no nation would *sacrifice its own*

THE EMOTIONAL BASIS OF HONOR

conception of right to it. By so doing it would renounce its highest ideals; it would allow its own sense of justice to be violated by an injustice and so dishonor itself."

If each nation has its own peculiar sense of honor therefore, it is not hard to see why any universal abstraction from such conflicting and variable data would be difficult, and this condition is indeed to be held responsible in great measure for the confusion in which the concept is steeped.

Still another variable element that has complicated the confusion is that nearly every man within the nation differs quantitatively and qualitatively with every other man in respect to his sensitiveness and understanding of honor. Just as there is variation as between nations, so there is variation within each nation as to what each member of it regards as matters affecting honor. If a questionnaire were sent out to representative men in the United States it would undoubtedly reveal a startling confusion and difference of opinion as to what subjects of our own foreign policy for example were properly to be classed as questions involving our honor. Some men believe that the subject of immigration bears directly upon it and that it should therefore at all costs be withheld from arbitration; others would refuse to admit disputes of this character to the precincts of non-arbitrable questions. If there are as many varieties of honor as there are nations to conceive it, it may be said with some exaggeration that there are likewise as many individual conceptions of each national honor as there are individuals to conceive it. No wonder that we must refrain from any attempt to define or universalize this confused and nondescript ideal if we wish to retain its sweeping emotional momentum.

The fact that rationality seems nevertheless to be attributed to honor in the apparently logical justifications which the ideal is so repeatedly given in every case in which national honor arises, does not alter the fact that strictly speaking honor has become an impulse, an emotion. Human nature takes what it wants emotionally, instinctively and without any previously deliberated recognition of the justice of its desire. Reason enters only as an "ex-post-facto justification." Frederick the Great used to say—"I begin by taking; later I shall find pedants to show that I was quite within my rights." So human nature might be said to feel a similar assurance instinctively, i.e., that rational justification will automatically follow upon the expression of the most purely emotional impulses.

This attempted rational justification in the case of national honor is the more surprising in view of the fact that it is generally recognized as an emotion by the very men who so try to defend it. The pre-rational character of the emotion of honor is, when it is regarded as a detached psychological problem, almost universally admitted; yet in spite of this admission men go on to explain the rationality of it just the same. The position is illustrated by Mr. Gilbert Murray who, starting from the premise that honor is a "sentiment not to be justified in reason" proceeds nevertheless to eulogize it as a rational ideal on the very same page on which he admits its essentially emotional character. If the purpose of this quotation were to point out merely an accidental contradiction, it would have been omitted, but this stand, impossible as it is, is almost generally assumed by men who talk of honor. When frankly put to them they usually admit that it is an emotion, but this does not seem to vitiate the ethical and rational defense which they go on to present in the same breath. By a mental somersault the ex-post-facto justification is taken out of its chronological order and assumed to be the preconceived rational incentive and stimulus of the emotional activity.

Mr. Gilbert Murray says—

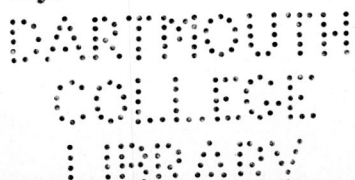

"A deal of nonsense no doubt is talked about honor and dishonor. *They are feelings based on sentiment not on reason.* The standards by which they are judged are often conventional or shallow and sometimes utterly false. Yet honor and dishonor are real things. *I will not try to define them,* but will only notice that like religion their characteristic is that they admit of no bargaining. Indeed we can almost think of honor as being that which a free man values more than life, and dishonor as that which he avoids more than suffering or death. And the important point for us is that there are such things.

"There are some people, followers of Tolstoi who accept this position so far as dying is concerned, but will have nothing to do with killing. Passive resistance they say is right; martyrdom is right; but to resist violence by violence is sin.

"I was once walking with a friend and disciple of Tolstoi's in a country lane; and a little girl was running in front of us. I put to him the well-known question—'Suppose you saw a man wicked or drunk or mad, run out and attack that child. You are a big man and carry a big stick; would you not stop him and if necessary knock him down?'

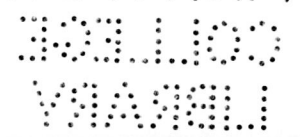

"'No,' he said; 'why should I commit a sin? I would try to persuade him, I would stand in his way, I would let him kill me, but I would not strike him.'

"Some few people will always be found, less than one in a thousand to take this view. They will say, 'Let the little girl be killed or carried off; let the wicked man commit another wickedness; I at any rate will not add to the mass of useless violence that I see all around me.'

"With such persons one cannot reason though one can often respect them. Nearly every normal man will *feel* that the real sin, the real dishonor lies in allowing an abominable act to be committed under your eyes while you have the strength to prevent it." ("Faith, War and Policy," p. 26.)

Here we have the frank admission that honor impulses are "feelings based on sentiment not on reason." In the next breath Mr. Murray assumes these impulses can and ought to be rationally defended.

When the fallacy is not the common one of separating the recognition of the emotional quality of honor from an independent rational justification, it is often the equally untenable fallacy of attributing an ethical *"tone"* to what is conceded to be impulsive conduct. The admittedly unrationalized emotion is by some strange logic nevertheless erected into an apotheosis of pure reason and eulogized as such. When the discrepancy is pointed out between the admission of honor as an emotion, and the justification of it as a rational ideal, men shrink from the inevitable inference that suggests itself and usually will go on to show the "holiness of instinct." Mr. Rumelin in his suggestive little work on "Politics and the Moral Law" says for example,

"It is well-known and perhaps a fortunate fact that we are not dependent upon the keenness and clearness of our reasoning faculty alone to teach us what we ought and ought not to do. We have an inner guide in those natural impulses which spontaneously cause us to turn in one direction or another. Though not infallible these impulses are seldom entirely wrong, and we find that not infrequently blind tact gives answer to the most difficult and complicated questions long before the wisdom of the wise has found a solution. On the other hand when we attempt to analyze these impulses we seem to be in a position similar to that of a somnambulist who having walked with a sure step upon dark and dangerous ways is suddenly awakened, and stops confused and helpless, not knowing how and whence he came. . . . Is politics, i.e., the untrammeled practice, of public affairs, subject to the moral

THE EMOTIONAL BASIS OF HONOR 95

law, or does it follow laws of its own?" (p. 24).

The admission of honor as an emotion or sentiment runs side by side in political literature with elaborate ethical and rational defenses of it. Herman Merivale in the second edition of his work "Colonization," (p. 675), stresses the importance of honor which "statesmen cannot disregard" and calls it an "impulse."

"To retain or abandon a dominion is not an issue which will ever be determined on the mere balance of profit or loss, not on the more refined but even less powerful motives supplied by abstract political philosophy. *The sense of National Honor;* the pride of blood, the tenacious spirt of self-defense, the sympathies of kindred communities, the instincts of a dominant race, the vague but generous desire to spread one's civilization and our religion over the world; these are IMPULSES which the student in his closet may disregard, but the statesman does not." (1861)

At the risk of appearing over-rational and of apparently ignoring the æsthetic appeal which honor makes to every normally constituted man, my object in this work is to show that by all tests which can be applied, honor as it is popularly conceived, is strictly speaking, an emotion, with only irrelevant rational accretions—which do not essentially belong to the ideal but which in the course of development have grown to be a part of it.

Though I believe that honor is an emotion, I do not mean to contend that that in itself is sufficient reason for deprecating it or for ignoring its commands. Emotions are the creative forces of life and are at the base of every humanitarian activity, every work of art, all invention, science and literature. But when we admit this we are using the word emotion in a very unscientific way to mean the most general constructive forces of human nature. For the purpose of this work it is necessary to distinguish between emotions that accompany constructive instincts such as the parental instinct, and those that accompany destructive instincts such as pugnacity and fear, at the same time keeping distinct such a midway instinct as self-assertion which is both. If honor were a distillation of the constructive instincts and manifested itself only in such legitimate expressions as defense of hearth and home, justice, humanity and other elevated aspirations, the assertion and proof that it is essentially an emotion would be nothing in its disfavor. It is true that a political concept is in bad taste when it is purely an emotion, but if that were the only objection here, honor might well afford to remain in all its sacred emotional glamor; for the end, ie., righteousness and humanity, would more than justify the means that attained them.

If, on the other hand, it has, as I maintain, grown, through misuse, to be largely the accompanying emotion of the destructive instincts and impulses of human nature, such as hatred, pugnacity, fear, suspicion, greed, and the small-boy-chip-on-the-shoulder attitude; then this honor is not a beautiful thing to be left in emotional obscurity and allowed to work havoc with our civilization. The honor which made America go to war in defense of Cuba was a result of the constructive parental instinct (McDougall's classification) working on a national scale and therefore hardly to be deprecated. But a war of conquest which is the outgrowth of the instinct of acquisitiveness is the much more frequent expression of honor, and this cannot be said to be beautiful or holy simply because it is an emotion.

When that which is regarded as an ethical ideal loses its essentially reasonable character, and the blind residual feeling becomes the motive force for the inception and perpetuation of the greatest crime of civilization, it is no longer a beautiful thing to be respected, but a criminal taint to be wiped out by all the relentless forces of logic.

CHAPTER V

TESTING FOR RATIONALITY

Honor can not be rational unless it can be shown that it has been conceived at least largely by reason and unless its modus operandi and expressions can be justified in reason. All action becomes rational only when the end is clearly apprehended and the means to attain that end calmly calculated before hand. These are so clearly conceived that the recognition of them induces action and actuates the will. That is to say, the action of emotion may more accurately be described as a yielding; rational conduct usually requires an effort which is sustained by a recognition of the objective goal. If honor is to be admitted into the domain of reason, its activity must embrace a deliberate consideration of the means and the consequences of what is to be brought about; and in this process it cannot violate any of the logical requirements demanded of other reasonable conceptions and activities.

At the outset, we are forced to concede that at best the "end" of honor is very vaguely conceived.

Before a thing can be said to be conceived it must admit of at least approximate definition. Definition is only another way of labeling the end. The impossibility of defining honor even in the most unsatisfactory way is evident from the fact that the Second Hague Conference deliberately avoided this embarrassing task. A review of the conflicting and confused utterances contained in the Symposium attest the nebulous and elusive character of it. It is elastic, vague and all-embracing and consequently even the most general definition would do violence to common usage. Insistence upon definition or enunciation of an ideal supposedly rational is not a rigorous test; it is the most legitimate test that can be applied to determine rationality. No one would think of admitting that the duty a husband owes to his wife, or a father to his son, or our ideal of honesty, or justice, or in fact any of our moral ideals, can not be satisfactorily defined. Ideals can be fully justified in reason and to ask this for honor is not to be exacting. Yet national honor begs to be excused from the difficult task of defending itself in the Court of Reason and through its speechless embarrassment stands self-convicted. The mass of contradictory expressions which are gathered together elsewhere, and which would be the legitimate material for

TESTING FOR RATIONALITY

definition, only emphasizes its irrational character.

This difficulty with regard to definition makes men naturally avoid asking pointed questions about it. In fact there has been so consistent a recognition of this evasiveness on the part of statesmen that few have dared to do so, perhaps out of compliance with a sort of "gentleman's agreement." In the case of personal honor we have passed the stage where people are timid about asking for a reasonable defense of it in each peculiar case, but we have not yet arrived at the point when a man is able to answer the question without feeling a slight suggestion of having compromised himself thereby. The following illustration taken from a popular magazine story is typical of this delicate evasiveness.

"I am a gentleman."

"Oh, are you? How amusing. How very amusing to be a gentleman and not a man. I suppose that is what it means to be a gentleman; to have no thought outside your career."

"Outside my honor none."

"And might I ask what is your honor?" She spoke in extreme irony.

"Yes, you may ask," he replied coolly. "But if you don't know without being told, I am afraid that I cannot explain it."

In the case of nations it is clear that opposition to all inclusive arbitration treaties arises from the fact that honor cannot be defined, and that therefore there are no standards or criteria by which it can be fairly judged and arbitrated. So long as honor comprises such a multiplicity of confused ends, it cannot be classified as a rational ideal. Not only is the end of honor as an abstraction, vague, but the end of honor in any specific dispute is equally obscure. The fact that a nation is unanimous in such cases, is no indication of its obvious rationality, or of the fact that every individual who so stoutly wishes to defend his country's honor, knows just what that honor happens to consist in at the time. In fact it makes little difference to him, for the patriotic attitude is, "My country right or wrong." One of our most prominent publicists states this position in unequivocal terms.

"In the place of the old motto, 'my country right or wrong,' we are told that we should adopt that other motto, 'My country when right and when wrong to be put right.' But who is to be judge as between you and your country? Is it the full measure of patriotic citizenship to be for your country when it agrees with you and against it when it does not? I cannot so estimate the impulses of loyalty. In the great tribunal of

TESTING FOR RATIONALITY 103

public opinion I shall strive always to bring my countrymen to the adoption of my views, but if their judgment differing from mine becomes the basis for national action and the cause of national conflict, I can find no satisfaction in the triumph of my country's foe; neither logic nor pride of opinion will soften the pain with which I greet the death of its defenders; with all my heart and soul and hopes and prayers, I am *always* for my country and its victory; and in no other spirit do I see aught but discord, the dissolution of allegiance and the death of loyalty."

Since patriotism demands that a country's honor must be defended regardless or whether the honor be based upon right or wrong, it is not surprising that men should be unwilling to inquire into the validity of the specific case. A rational recognition of his country in the wrong would perhaps take a little of his zest away, and this must not be allowed in any event, for it is my country's honor, right or wrong. This is not a case of reductio ad absurdum but a simple case of accepting the most obvious inference following upon this position. When men go to war, though they know their country to be wrong rationally, it is not human nature for them to really believe so. Their country is right even when it is wrong and honorable even in its dishonor.

Tennyson's paradox gives us this moral confusion.

> "His honor rooted in dishonor stood,
> And faith unfaithful kept him falsely true."

It is no wonder that in all this moral confusion an attempt at definition is a delicate task and has been consistently avoided.

If honor cannot and need not be defined, there is obviously no need of universalizing it. But universality is a prerequisite of rationality. Given the assumption that it is wrong for France to violate Belgian neutrality, then it is equally wrong for England to do so. Or if it is wrong for Germany to impose its form of government on England then it is wrong for England to commit the same offense upon Germany. Rational ideals are universal and if they do not work in every situation they at least must work both ways.

The test of universality shows honor to be irrational. For example England demanded to be consulted in the Morocco treaty but unreasonably refused to allow Germany this privilege; and the interesting thing is that she defended these contradictory positions by insisting that they were both obligations of her national honor. (See Symposium.) Germany to-day would be perfectly willing to dominate other races, but she would rather be wiped off the map than submit to domination. In fact the whole principle of this aspect of honor consists in a recognition that another nation will submit to what we would never submit. In fact because honor lacks the quality of universality, it is nothing more than a dignified expression of the simple rule of right which a Mohammedan once enunciated. When asked what was right, he replied, "It is right for me to take my neighbor's wife." "And wrong?" "For my neighbor to take my wife," he returned sharply.

The application of our rational ideals can not stop at rivers and mountains. And likewise the mere difference in the particular object of a national mission does not alter the universal fact that spreading such missions by force is either wrong in every case or wrong in no case.

Another fallacy is committed in what might be called the granted premise. The error of "begging the question" is perhaps the most frequent and persistent in the discussion of honor disputes. The men who would suppress all opposition to a proposed war even going so far as physical violence, defend their extreme measures on the theory that a man who will not uphold the honor of his country is a traitor, and that no punishment is adequate for him. This may be true, but the premise which is taken for granted in condemning such men, is the very thing which the alleged traitor refuses to admit, namely, that in the war proposed, genuine honor is at stake. The whole justification for his stand is that the point at issue does not involve rational honor; but militarists and patriots refuse to meet such pacifists on the plane of this premise, and rail against them on the unfair assumption that they will not fight for honor. Voltaire has well said that much discussion could be obviated if men only defined their positions.

The following quotation from Lord Russell represents this fallacy, in a slightly different way.

"That (Alabama claims) is a question of honor which we will not arbitrate, for England's honor can never be made the subject of arbitration."

Now the premise which was taken for granted here and not argued out on its own merits, is that the Alabama claims was a question of honor. Nobody thought of asking the question at the time—"Are the Alabama claims something which offends British honor?" That was taken for granted just as all such statements made by the "custodians of the national honor" are taken on faith. The argument and interest never revolve about the genuineness or falseness of the point of honor, but about the question whether it ought to be resented or arbitrated. The very ring of the sentence—"That is a question of honor which we will never arbitrate for *England's honor can never be made the subject of arbitration,*" suggests where the psychological stress really lies. If there is any debate it may possibly be in connection with the wisdom of arbitrating the honor; but the peremptory tone of the first part of the sentence—"that is a question of honor which we will not arbitrate"—precludes all rational questioning on that score.

This granted premise creeps in so quietly, especially when men are being swayed by Chauvinism, that it is not noticed, and if some very skeptical individual does observe it, he wisely keeps his mouth shut.

An exact parallel of this fallacy is given by James who draws this illustration of an irrational process containing a granted premise.

"Suppose I say when offered a piece of cloth, —'I won't buy that; it looks as if it would fade'; —meaning merely that something about it suggests the idea of fading to my mind. My judgment though possibly correct is not reasoned but purely empirical; but if I can say that into the color there enters a certain dye which I know to be chemically unstable, and that therefore the color will fade, my judgment is reasoned."

In excluding from its jurisdiction disputes involving honor the Hague in a somewhat similar way took for granted, as needing no justification, the very thing which, above all other material of international discord, needed to be defined.

The definition of honor was taken for granted, and no one at the Conference dared to ask for enlightenment on this very interesting point. The same timidity which is shown by ordinary citizens toward the question—"Does this dispute involve our honor?"—was shown by the delegates at the Hague toward the question—"What is national honor?" Both these questions show a spirit of cold calculation toward a sentiment that is woven into the emotional and æsthetic nature of men. The only way in which one may show a proper appreciation of the sentiments, therefore, is not to question the validity of any of the premises upon which it rests. The sentiment makes a very strong dramatic appeal and to look beneath this brings upon the earnest thinker the stigma of cowardice and disloyalty. Men respond only to the dramatic quality of honor and since this quality reaches its highest expression on an emotional foundation, it is no wonder that men should care little about rational justification. Honor may be rooted in dishonor, yet it has the same beauty as if it were planted in the Garden of Eden. It is like a castle in the air; we see its beauty entirely disconnected from a substantial foundation. A foundation is taken for granted; if it is not there, an improvised one can be erected; if that is impossible the castle appears to have sufficient buoyancy to hang in the air just the same. Honor appears to be its own justification; it is the end which in true Jesuit fashion sanctifies the means. . . . When the false premises are pointed out the structure does not fall but becomes stronger and firmer. The miracle which the Irishman expected to perform is attained here. Having piled a number of boxes on top of each other he found that he needed one more to reach the first story and so he suggested to his friend that they take the bottom box out and place it on the top.

Another difficulty is the readiness with which men draw inferences by automatic association. Honor and war have for centuries been inseparably associated, so that try as we may to associate peace and honor we have the neurone associations against us. Just as honor and war form one distinct associative process, so peace and cowardice form another, and reason though we may, the power of these automatic processes can not be decreased, and its influence on our thinking nullified. The recognition of this, therefore, gives the militarist a certain advantage in a dispute. The mechanical associations which spring up around honor are many and beautiful—courage, strength, sacrifice, national emblems, music, poetry, and all the æsthetic and emotional ramifications of these. But the thought of an honorable peace makes no such automatic connections.

I will have more to say on this point of the attractiveness of honor through mental and emotional associations elsewhere, but for the present it is only necessary to admit the demoralizing influence of these automatic associations upon the rational quality of the ideal. When a subject must be judged on the merits and logic of each case, it is necessary if we wish our inference to be genuine, to approach the case without bias or prejudice. In so far as we approach it with such bias our judgment must necessarily be colored. We must strip our minds of these accretions of automatic associations if we wish to attain to a really reasoned judgment.

The foolishness of this inveterate association of honor and war becomes obvious when we con-

TESTING FOR RATIONALITY

sider that in almost every war either one or both sides were, according to the judgment of history, wrong. The axiomatic truth which we must draw from this, is that a nation stands an equal chance of being wrong and of its true honor lying more rationally with the alternative of peace. But in spite of the equal liability to error which every nation should feel in every dispute that may arise, the automatic processes are altogether on the side of the war alternative, with the absoluteness of infallibility. With such a psychological handicap it is no wonder that men cannot approach each case in a scientific spirit and accept the impersonal conclusion which a free and unfettered intellect might be compelled to draw.

Having assured ourselves that honor has none of the distinguishing ear-marks of a rational ideal, we will consider the only alternative which is left—whether it has any or all of the distinctive traits of an emotion.

CHAPTER VI

TESTING FOR AN EMOTION

THE tests applied in the last chapter prove with a fair amount of conclusiveness that honor is not a rational concept by any psychological test that can be applied; that it lacks the most essential characteristics of rationality both in the way it is conceived, and in the mode of its expression. And in determining its irrational quality we have laid the foundations for determining what it must as the only alternative be, that is, an emotion; for the first requisite of emotion is irrationality. It will appear that just as honor lacks every characteristic of a rational concept, it contains every quality of an emotion.

Next to irrationality, the most characteristic thing about emotion is uniformity, or unanimity of reaction to a given situation among any large group of people. When millions of people confined within one set of geographical boundaries, can agree among themselves and at the same time disagree diametrically with millions of people within another set of boundaries, it is difficult to

TESTING FOR AN EMOTION

explain the uniformity within the two opposing camps in any other way than as being due to the contagion of emotion. The fervor with which every Englishman but Russell is convinced that Germany ought to be crushed; the accord with which every German but Liebknecht cries, "Gott Strafe England;" the certainty with which every Frenchman but Rolland regards Germany as the aggressor; these instances of unanimous conviction emphasize the extreme mental vigor that is required to detach oneself from the influence of national consciousness, and prove that national assurance in a war of national honor is not based upon reason which is peculiar to the individual, but inspired by emotion which is common to all. On questions of science, religion, morality, law, men following their rational impulses are divided; on matters of honor there is always within any country a unanimous bias. This is not an accident of rational uniformity, but the inevitable result of emotional infection. If such unanimity happened within the confines of a country once or twice it would even then be stretching a point to regard it as the mere coincidence arising from independent judgments. But when a country is known to be one and to present a united front in every war of honor; when differences of opinion on resenting honor offenses are almost non-existent; when Congresses and Reichstags vote to defend honor by unanimous assent, we can no longer depend upon the law of chance to explain the alignment of independent rational judgments into such solid geographical phalanxes. Thought is not contagious; if it were some of our most serious educational problems would be solved.

What is wanted in a nation in time of crisis is action, and action cannot be secured as a result of critical conflicting thought. The prerequisite to effective action is unanimity and unanimity can only be achieved through the medium of the emotions and feelings. And though we may agree that national efficiency in the sense of accomplishing an object independently of its justice or injustice, wisdom, or foolishness, requires unanimity, the explanation of this unanimity of thought on the basis of accident, is nevertheless inadequate.

How much more easily this uniformity is explained when we think of honor as an emotion. Given an emotional situation and it can be safely predicted that every normal man and child will react in exactly the same way with only slight difference in the degree of reaction due to individual peculiarity. The contact with a slimy wrig-

TESTING FOR AN EMOTION

gly thing will almost universally inspire an emotion of disgust. Equally, every normal person will feel the tender emotion of protection toward a child that is being mistreated. The basic appeal of literature, drama, music, in fact, all art, is its emotional quality which calls forth a universal and inevitable response. Even when we have decided that rationally it is better not to yield to certain impulses, such as helping an unworthy beggar, we still react uniformly and resist with an effort, if we do resist, the impulse which we cannot help feeling nevertheless.

The instinct which explains this uniformity of emotional response to what is admittedly an intellectual problem, is the gregarious instinct, "the consciousness of kind." The gregarious instinct kills more independent thinking than all the bad intellectual processes of our school systems. Under the influence of this powerful instinct men either *unconsciously* fall into line with the general attitude without reasoning on their own part, gravitating toward the current attitude emotionally; or they fall into line consciously though they disapprove of the popular trend, preferring to violate promptings of their own reason, rather than to ignore the incessant tugging at the heart to follow the crowd. In the one case reason does not enter at all, and in the other it is forcibly expelled when it does enter. In both cases the result is unanimity.

Professor Giddings regards the "consciousness of kind" as the basic principle of social organization. He says—

"In its widest extension the consciousness of kind marks off the animate from the inanimate. Within the wide class of the animal it marks off species from races. Within racial lines the consciousness of kind underlies the more definite ethical and political groupings, it is the basis of class distinctions, of innumerable forms of alliances, of rules of intercourse and of peculiarities of policy. Our conduct toward those whom we feel to be most like ourselves is instinctively and rationally different from our conduct towards others, whom we believe to be less like ourselves. Again it is the consciousness of kind and nothing else, which distinguishes social conduct as such from purely economic, and purely political or purely religious conduct, for in actual life it constantly interferes with the theoretically perfect operation of the economic, political, or religious motive. The workingman joins a strike of which he does not approve rather than cut himself off from his fellows. For a similar reason the man-

TESTING FOR AN EMOTION

ufacturer who questions the value of protection to his own industry yet pays his contribution to the protectionist campaign fund. The southern gentleman who believed in the cause of the union, none the less threw in his fortunes with the confederacy, if he felt himself to be one of the Southern people and a stranger to the people of the North. The liberalizing of creeds is accomplished by the efforts of men who are no longer able to accept the traditional dogma, but who desire to maintain associations which it would be painful to sever. *In a word it is about the consciousness of kind that all other motives organize themselves, in the evolution of social choice, social volition, or social policy."*

The salient thing about this "consciousness of kind" is that it is emotional; that it operates in the dim and shadowy orbs of emotional associations, carrying as satellites to it, rational accretions and philosophic speculations. We need but to take an extreme case to see that the rational explanations follow in the wake of this emotional consciousness of kind with its deadening influence on thought. Mr. Stewart Chamberlain's book which sets out to prove that everything worth while that was ever accomplished in the world, had a Teutonic origin, is a position which has many emotional adherents in Germany, and is changing the geographical origin of perfection in many other countries.

The conclusion therefore is that the unanimity which we invariably see within countries when "honor is at stake," is not due to any uniform recognition of justice either through the instrument of reason or divine revelation, but that it is due to the deadening influence of the gregarious instinct upon independent thinking. This unanimity must have an emotional cause, for unanimity is one of the most important characteristics of an emotion.

Directness of response to stimuli, which is another characteristic of honor, is also a quality of emotion, not of reason. Rationally we stop to think before acting, no matter for how short an interval. But in the case of honor we resent directly. Honor insults are not resented after careful thought and deliberation. It is not the thought of the offense which makes us resent, but it is the apprehension of the offense itself which directly arouses our resentment without the interposition of any thought or conscious process at all. Some reasonable activity may follow directly after the resentment is spontaneously aroused, but this is not to say that reason in any way enters in the apprehension of the offense.

TESTING FOR AN EMOTION

In other words we do not want to strike because we think of the abstraction of honor, but we think of the abstraction of honor because we feel the impulse to strike.

In fact the more directly, that is to say the more immediately, an offense to honor is resented and the less the consideration or thought introduced between the time the offense is received and the time that it is resented, the more virile and honorable a nation is felt to be. In other words the quality of the honor deteriorates in direct proportion to the amount of time which is allowed for the purpose of thoughtful consideration to elapse, between the time of offense and the time of vindication. Consequently a nation which pauses to examine the offense, to determine whether it is real or fancied, must, according to the ideal be fundamentally deficient in the quality of its national honor.

This melodramatic quality of immediate resentment to offenses of honor, of spontaneous and instantaneous yielding to impulse, is, except for the point of unanimity above mentioned, the most fundamental and characteristic thing about all emotions. Emotion seeks its expression instinctively and without thought. Men do not fall in love, strike when offended, or protect a helpless child out of an intellectual choice in the matter; nor is it to satisfy their desire for a preconceived end. They do these things in direct response to certain pre-rational pushes which are woven into the fabric of their natures. One may be thrown into a paroxysm of fear by the appearance of a white sheet in the night though he know positively that no harm can come to him from it. And so the fact that an honor activity is an immediate expression in response to a stimulus, places it automatically in the category of emotion.

In this connection it is common knowledge that the less rational a man becomes, the more sensitive does his honor become, and the quicker does he react to a real or imaginary insult. If we could apply an anæsthetic to the rational faculty of a man we would find that he would be governed by his "honor" impulses in direct proportion to the amount of anæsthetic administered. While such an experiment would be difficult, we can see that this is true by examining the case of a drunkard which is as nearly a case of numbed rationality as we can reasonably find. There is no one more sensitive and melodramatic about his honor than a drunkard. The least slight, the most casual aspersion upon his ambition or his character, the most guarded intima-

TESTING FOR AN EMOTION

tion that he is drunk—all these things send the flush to his cheek, and wound his honor. And, yet psychologists tell us that drunkenness is the let-down of all the rational and intellectual checks, and a complete yielding to impulse. The sensitiveness of honor therefore can have no relation to the clarity of reason, but obviously depends upon emotionalism. We associate the following expression of melodramatic honor for example, more commonly with a bar-room than with a co-educational college, let us say—

"If you touch that woman, I'll kill you."

In the same way the idiot who is totally unable to interpose any reasoning between the reception of an offense to his honor and his vindication of it, for the obvious reason that he has none to interpose, is nevertheless very sensitive about his honor. He responds and responds directly because his idiocy does not weaken the emotional springs from which honor draws its sustenance. The story is told of an idiot in the N. Y. State Insane Asylum who was insulted by a warden and as a result has refused to have anything to do with any one who comes to visit him. From the day he was insulted, which was about fifteen years ago, until to-day, he has persistently refused to talk to any one, so that he has by this time probably lost all power of speech. Such was the delicacy and sensitiveness of his sense of honor.

Another important quality of emotional activity and one which follows as a corollary to "direct response," is intolerance. A Supreme Court judge who may differ very vitally from his associates in a matter of justice will not throw himself into a panic of fury or intolerance if he is careful to preserve his judicial calm. Open-mindedness, unlike "closed-heartedness," is never intolerant of a difference of opinion. Guided by reason solely a nation could not in justice take the position that all who disagreed with it were wrong. A rational man grants his liability to error in every dispute. Reason is admittedly fallible, but emotion, to judge from the positive expressions which it assumes, is the apotheosis of infallibility. There is no one more impatient or intolerant than a man or a nation whose honor has been wounded. Then it is not the time to argue, to compromise, to hesitate or to reason; it is time to strike. Not only do nations refuse to listen to explanations from without, but they show an unreasonable intolerance toward opposition from within. The suppression of such opposition is not justly explained by the fact that men coolly recognize the inefficiency of a country divided against itself. They may build up this justification later, but at the moment they are intolerant because the emotion which has been roused is intolerant. It is this intolerance which leads not only to war, but which manifests itself as well in riots and in forcible suppression of views contrary to popular opinion. It is not surprising that the jingo should use upon his compatriots as well as his enemies, the logic of force as his instrument of persuasion. The same emotions which make him intolerant to heed the justice of the enemy country, makes him intolerant to see the other side of the controversy in his own country. His emotions are reasonable enough to be consistently irrational. The reason that those who are not influenced by the emotional "honor" stimulus, are comparatively tolerant, is because their sustaining force is calm reason. The "honor" champion is buoyed along by the emotional forces of hatred, fear, self-assertion; and it is no wonder that having this backing he is so sure of himself and of his strength; so intolerant of his antagonist.

The James-Lange test of an emotion can not be applied to national honor for the simple reason that the nation can not be said to have the physical manifestation of the individual. But if we regard military power as the collateral physical manifestation of the national emotion, just as the increased heart beat and blood pressure are the physical manifestations of individual emotions, we can draw an interesting parallel. The James-Lange theory maintains that the intensity of an emotional state depends directly upon its physical expressions, in fact that the emotion is the sum total of these expressions; and that if it were possible to subtract the physical ear-marks, the emotion would be lost entirely. For example, if we could stop the increased blood-pressure, the tenseness of the muscles, and the strained eyes in the case of anger, we would find that in spite of the existence of an adequate stimulus, we would no longer feel the emotion.

In just this way if we subtracted the single tangible manifestation of a nation that accompanies great national emotions, that is to say, its military power, we would find that the emotion of national honor would no longer exist in the same sense in which it exists to-day. And it would not disappear because of a *conscious* recognition of military incapacity to sustain it. It would disappear automatically. Honor will keep, and has kept direct pace with national "visceral" change of military power, and inversely. In fact the application of the James-Lange test suggests the following generalization which might be termed the Law for National Honor.

The sensitiveness and intensity of a nation's honor increases directly with a recognition of its relative military strength, and inversely with the consciousness of the strength of an opposing military power.

A country which is decidedly weaker than another, by the instinct of self-preservation, becomes more reflective about the type of honor offenses which ought to be resented by war. In the preliminaries of the Franco-Prussian War, Bismark never felt for a moment that Germany's honor was at stake in the wrangle over the Spanish candidature, until his War Minister Von Roon assured him that Germany was in a position to overcome Napoleon's forces. It is a historical fact that for a time Germany was not so sure of its relatively stronger army. But when the time came, though the dispute was not changed, and was still the candidacy to the Spanish throne, Bismarck changed the Ems dispatch and created a point of honor for the occasion by making it appear that the French minister had insulted the Kaiser. In his "Errinerungen und Gedanken" he admits having artificially created a point of honor when the army was ready.

But in most cases the process is not so calmly

intellectualized, but works instinctively. A country like Holland will naturally have less of an exacting sense of honor than Germany, that is when the latter is involved in some dispute with Germany; but toward Siam, Holland might become extremely exacting about punctilios of honor. It is true that even a comparatively small nation like Belgium felt its honor to be uncompromising and inviolable even as against such a mighty nation as Germany. But here the point was clear and fundamental—the inviolability of her territory; a thing which she had declared to the world she would regard as an obligation of honor. And in order to live up to her honor, Belgium disregarded the most primary instincts of self-preservation, and invited annihilation. This is certainly an exceptional case and can be regarded as the exception to prove the rule, that honor varies with the recognition of relative military strength or weakness. Luxemburg, which was bound by a similar convention, did not resist Germany's invasion but allowed the armies to pass through her territory.

In its foreign relations, there is a tendency on the part of the nation who has the giant's power, to use it like a giant; and to do this not out of a recognition of the discrepancy in military power between it and its opponent, but instinctively and unconsciously. We find Germany's sense of honor increasing in delicacy with her growing sense of power until in 1907 the Kaiser declared that it was a "matter of honor" now that Germany had "become a world power," to be consulted "in any future exploitation of the globe" and in the "making of any and all treaties." In the days of Napoleon it is not speculation to say that Prussia would honestly not have felt so ambitious a sense of national honor.

In fact psychology helps us in this theory which I maintain, namely, that in the face of peril nations do not feel the emotion of honor. In a situation of genuine peril there is an instinctive tendency to think more clearly and dismiss emotion. Here the law of self-preservation comes in, for it is clear that those people who in the face of danger had given way to emotion would by the law of survival have been eliminated. A man in a burning building will very often calculate calmly the best way to escape instead of throwing himself into a paroxysm of fear. The complete instinct of self-preservation overcomes mere fragments of itself, of which all the other instincts and emotions may properly be considered, for the whole is bigger and stronger than any of its parts.

The McDougall test for an emotion—hypertrophy, or pathological abnormalities, bears out the point that honor is an emotion. Hypertrophy of the honor sentiment is quite common.

His other test; namely, that the rudimentary beginnings of a fundamental emotion may be found in lower animals, is illustrated by the fact that a dog for example can be insulted, and will snarl around with his tail between his legs until he has either vindicated what might be analogously termed canine honor, or until he has been reconciled.

In the case of nations, the honor emotion has often become hypertrophied and grotesquely exaggerated. The meglomania and passion for world dominion which Napoleon felt was a pathological expression of honor. Everything was done for "L'honneur et la gloire de la patrie." And to-day "Deutchtum" with its pathological craving for world domination is, too, a grotesque, dramatic perversion of "Deutsche Ehre," for there is no country in the world which has used the slogan of honor in so many bizarre connections.

The above illustrations of pathological exag-

TESTING FOR AN EMOTION

geration are really abnormal to the second degree for the reason that normally a man or a nation is not conscious of honor at all. The man in the streets, except in times of war or crisis, never feels or talks about his country's honor. It is only when an abnormal situation arises, and when he becomes abnormally stimulated and fired with a war-like patriotism, that he begins to feel it. So the McDougall test for an emotion is really doubly satisfied here.

There is only one way to account for the obviously false position which nations have under the cloak of honor assumed, positions which they themselves admitted later to have been false and unwarranted; namely, that when we feel emotion, we become blind to the most obvious facts, and our minds work in such a way as to preclude everything which might conflict with, or weaken the emotion that we feel. The fact that this is exactly what happens invariably in the case of honor, puts another emotional ear-mark upon it. The following observation made by the British psychologist Bain is pertinent at this point:

"In a state of strong excitement no thoughts are allowed to present themselves except such as concur in the present moods; the links of association are paralyzed as regards everything which conflicts with the ascendant influence; and it is through this stoppage of the intellectual trains that we come into the predicament of renouncing or as it is called disbelieving, for the moment what we have felt and acted on. Our feelings convert our convictions by smiting us with intellectual blindness. It depends upon many circumstances what intensity of emotion shall be required to produce this higher effect of keeping utterly back the faintest recollection of whatever discords with the reigning fury. The natural energy of the emotional temper on the one hand, and feebleness of the forces of effective resuscitation on the other, conspire to falsify the views entertained at the moment." (P. 21, "Emotion and Will.")

The fact that in honor disputes nations have really given up the obvious axiom of equal liability to error, can only be explained in the way that Bain asserts. The fact that England could have regarded the Opium War as a matter of honor, is a case in point. The power of "emotion to bar out the impression of reality," is one of the most fundamental truths in psychology.

"Intense emotions, while inspiring the actions, and influencing the intellectual acquisitions, likewise affect the judgment of true and false. The emotion of terror proves the greatness of its power by inducing the most irrational beliefs. In the extreme manifestations of anger, a man will be suddenly struck blind to his most familiar experiences of fact, and will for the moment deny what at other times he would most resolutely maintain. Take also self-complacency. The habitual dreamer is not instructed by a thousand failures of pet projects; he enters upon each new attempt as full of confidence as if all the rest had succeeded. We note with surprise that in every day life an individual goes on promising to himself and to others with sincere conviction what he has never once been known to execute; the feeling of self-confidence lords it over the experiences of life. He has not stated to himself in a proposition the conflicting experience. He does not know that he never fulfilled his purposes.—Also love's blindness is the world's oldest proverb." (Ibid., p. 21.)

Emotions are sometimes objectless; that is, they exist without any reasonable cause. We sometimes feel fear and do not know to what to refer it. Men suffering from acute indigestion often become frightened in a very serious way for no reason. Wand says in this connection:

"The moods of emotion to which we are at times subject are caused by bodily states; and it is in these cases that the cause to which they are due is so different from the object to which they come to be referred. For while the cause is some state of the body, the object is something we invent to complete and justify the emotion. For it does not satisfy us to feel an emotion and not to be able to refer it to anything in particular; and when a man is in an angry mood there is scarcely anything however unreasonable to which he may not attribute it." ("Foundations of Character," p. 199.)

Honor in just this way is known to float in the atmosphere as it were, with no anchorage, no particular resting place. A man often goes around with a chip on his shoulder for no reason but just "contrariness," and woe to the one who wounds his honor which at such times is exceedingly delicate. And so, a nation drunk with power, will carry a similar chip, and look for some convenient object to submerge with a torrent of honorable rage.

Putting all these tests together we must infer that expressions of honor require no effort of the will, as is the case with all purely rational judgments, but might be described as a "yielding." And it is only when we act thus emotionally that we ever speak of yielding.

The tests applied above prove that honor answers every prerequisite of an emotion.

CHAPTER VII

DISSECTING THE HONOR COMPLEX

In the preceding chapters I asserted somewhat dogmatically that the motive force of the sentiment of honor radiated from the emotion purely, and not from the intellectual element of the complex. By divorcing the two elements, and imagining each of them in various situations alone, it will be easier to determine experimentally just how much there is of truth in this theory. So long as the complex is considered as a unit, it is impossible to determine what proportion of directivity arises from the emotional and what from the pseudo-intellectual ingredients.

Now, if a man whose honor has been roused by these two inseparable elements, should suddenly for some reason lose the *justification,* that is the rational element from his consciousness, the emotional momentum will carry him on. The emotion is remembered long after the justification is forgotten, and just as it is born long before reason has had a chance to introduce it, so it remains long after reason has died away from it.

134 WHAT IS "NATIONAL HONOR"?

Suppose a situation in which a man's honor has been wounded and in which he later discovers that rationally he had no right to take offense. Does that loss of justification effect the emotional momentum which he feels nevertheless toward vindicating himself? Does the mere recognition that he had "no business being hurt" suffice and appease his anger? It is possible to reason with reason, but with emotion the task is much more difficult because emotion must be consistent even at the cost of being irrational. Once an emotion is roused, it will seek its expression, and will be swept along by its own momentum over any rational obstacles that suggest a turning back. Once it turns its hand to the plow emotion turns not backward to retrace its steps. We have so often heard the story of the father who decided to give his youngster a good licking for getting into a fight, and although he later found that the boy did not commit the offense, he licked him just the same because he had made up his mind to do so and wished to be consistent. On a national scale the Boer War furnishes us another illustration of this interesting point; namely that the loss of justification offers no embarrassment to emotion. England after having entered the Boer War found that the justification for her entrance had been built on mis-

DISSECTING THE HONOR COMPLEX

information. But she could not turn back. "Whatever good reason there may have been for recognizing that our (English) claims of sovereignty in the Transvaal rested on a mistaken view of native sentiment, and however fairly such recognition might have been allowed to affect the ultimate settlement, the game of war once entered upon ought to have been played out until it was either lost or won. To this the HONOR of the country was fully pledged." (H. I. D. Ryder in *Nineteenth Century*—referring to Boer War—1899.)

The emotion of honor carried England along "consistently," and in the face of this sweeping undercurrent, the mere recognition that she was persisting in a false and mistaken ideal, was powerless. At such times the intellect may in fact be so little affected as "to play the cold-blooded spectator" and note the absence of justification for the emotion.

We have frequent illustrations of the distinctness of the two elements, and of the fact that rationality does not affect the emotional aspect except in the case of the most strong-minded people. How often we hear an offended person say, even after a rational and adequate explanation has been given him by the offender; "But I can't help it if I feel hurt." The hurt has registered, and all the assurance in the world cannot remove the hurt nor the consequent irrational resentment of it. The mere circumstance of wiping away the intellectual side of the hurt, does not alter the emotional currents, because the two work independently, and it is only because the former takes its cue from the emotion, that there are so many happy coincidences.

That the emotion is the vital and sole force behind honor impulses we can see from the vestiges that remain of duel honor. A man who has been insulted, though he may think as most men do, that a "gentleman" is not supposed to fight, will nevertheless feel a very strong *impulse* to strike. He admits the good sense of giving up private vengeance in the interest of social order, but he cannot make himself *feel* the justice of it. The duel is still common in France and in Germany, especially among military students. These are merely illustrations of the difficulty which logic has in overcoming the emotional impulses upon which our conduct is so largely determined.

Honor, like art, becomes its own justification. To turn back, is never regarded as a recognition of the injustice which a country would commit by continuing, but as a confession of cowardice. This attitude is almost a tacit acceptance of the

DISSECTING THE HONOR COMPLEX

saying of Nietzsche, "a good war will sanctify a bad cause."

To take an instance from personal honor, let us suppose the case of a man who feels his sense of civic honor to be violated. Intellectually such an exposé as the Tweed affair some years ago in New York City, may have offended the civic honor of thousands of good citizens. So far as value to society and to the advancement of vital ideals is concerned, an offense to a man's civic honor might sensibly call forth a willingness to undergo almost any sacrifice. Yet the cold abstract recognition of the rottenness of the political corruption did not lead the outraged citizens to do more than cast their vote against the corrupt official at the next election, while less vigilant citizens may not even have done that. But an insult to the wife of any one of these men might have prompted him to any measure in her defense. In reason, it is not hard to see that that insult is not nearly so vital an offense to social ideals as public plunder. A man might conceivably give his life, as men so often did in the age of chivalry, to vindicate one honor impulse, and be unwilling to give one dollar to the Honest Ballot Association. The one offense arouses his emotion, which carries honor to any length in vindication, while the other arouses intellect, which is dead and lifeless for the purposes of stimulating action. Few feel an emotional vigor and intensity for the latter except in the rare cases where men have a "passion" for public service.

It is impossible to work upon an emotional correlative artificially, as William James says. "Just as an artificially imitated sneeze lacks something of the reality, so the attempt to imitate an emotion in the absence of the normal instigating cause is apt to be rather hollow."

Often when we have associated the rational justification with the emotion, we ourselves admit the stupidity of the justification when the emotion has cooled. I heard a great professor admit that he was ashamed of the imperialistic honor which he felt during McKinley's administration. When the emotion dies away the embarrassed pseudo-rational fragment is left out in the cold in all its naked unreasonableness and injustice.

CHAPTER VIII

THE TYRANNY OF A PHRASE

"There never were creatures of prey so mischievous, never diplomats so cunning, never poisons so deadly, as these masked words. They are the unjust stewards of all men's ideas. Whatever fancy or favorite instinct a man most cherishes he gives to his favorite masked words to take care of for him. The word at last comes to have an infinite power over him, and you can not get at him but by its ministry."

—JOHN RUSKIN.

It would seem that thought must precede language, determining our choice of words, and that the latter are merely symbols predetermined by the nature of the thought itself. But only too often the relationship is reversed and a word which has acquired a deep significance through various associations, will determine our thought regardless of the specific connection in which it is used. For example when the term honor is spoken, the specific associations of the moment disappear and are virtually submerged in a deluge of emotional respect for honor as an abstract principle. We approve the principle and by the strange logic of a transferred epithet we approve the point in the particular case, overlooking the necessity of deciding whether the particular issue raised really involves honor or not. We do not judge each case on its own merits but on the merits of the great national imperative which has come down to us as a beautiful tradition. All our thought and feeling seem to go not to an analysis of the dispute but to a worship of the ethical dogma.

Thus it has come about that the logical process whereby our thought fixes the labels, has been reversed. Our reason no longer works untrammeled and free from bias, because we are working as it were, inductively. Emotion shot through with subconscious experiences and associations bearing upon the general principle, formulate a justification for us in every case which our reason is later compelled to support. With a sort of a priori vengeance, emotion and bias cast the die into which we pour a rational justification.

This has come to be true of the phrase "national honor" which, by filling us with an emotional thrill, calls forth not only a spontaneous intellectual approval, no matter in what connection it arises, but also a deliberate moral justification, even though conventional morality must be torn to shreds in the process. It makes little difference whether a nation invokes the term honor in defense of a crime or an ideal; the essential sacredness of the term remains. When a country connects honor with aggression, the unthinking patriot feels only the honor and is blind to the aggression. The term has become hallowed and consecrated by the centuries of blood and suffering which it has called forth since men first began to fight for honor. The vehemence of hatred caused by repeated wars, the sacrifice in life and money, the intensity of pain and suffering, the glories, and the progress of civilization which is attributed to war, have been transferred to the term honor and have filled the phrase itself with an intense fervor and a sacred glamor. In the face of these emotional ramifications reason is paralyzed. We have transferred the cumulative emotion of a series of intense experiences to the term national honor, so that it has become a tyrannous phrase invested with the magic power to shape our moral thinking. Instead of attempting to strip the term of its unwarranted suggestiveness at this late stage of its involution, we have long since made a fetish of it at which we kneel blindly in worship.

When the psychological tyranny of the phrase is brought into question, it is easy to escape the necessity for rational analysis by taking refuge in the ideal of national honor as an abstract principle. From a psychological tyrant it then becomes an intellectual despot, a sort of categorical imperative to which reason and good sense must submit. Loyalty to an abstract principle, regardless of specific applications is doubtful morality, especially when, as is often the case with an adherence to the abstraction of honor, such loyalty defeats the very purposes for which the ideal is supposed to exist.

There is yet another factor which lends strength to this tyranny, and that is the very indefiniteness of the honor abstraction. An abstraction is tyrannical even when its power can be limited by definition. A principle is always absolute, while incidents are relative; so that adherence to the principle usually does violence to the experiences which it governs. But when a definition of an abstraction and its implications is impossible as is the case with honor, its power necessarily becomes unlimited, in direct proportion to its vagueness. It would seem that a principle must, by its very function as a guide to conduct, be a *definite criterion* by which particular incidents can be judged. It does not appear unreasonable then to expect that this criterion by which the right or wrong of specific in-

THE TYRANNY OF A PHRASE

cidents are defined should itself admit of definition. But national honor defies analysis in direct proportion to the absoluteness with which it tyrannizes over a situation.

The attitude of men toward honor therefore, becomes a matter of "loyalty to loyalty," or loyalty for loyalty's sake, rather than loyalty to an ideal involved in a specific case. The loyalty has become so intense as to overlook completely the necessity for rational ideals. It has become an absolute devotion to the principle of "dying for *an ideal*." The average man who is willing to die for the ideal of national honor is only concerned with the element of loyalty, which he feels to be the only element in true patriotism. He is wholly indifferent to the character of the ideal for it is "my country right or wrong." He seldom stops to consider that ideal living might better serve his purpose than ideal dying.

The ethical justification of dying for an ideal is three-fold. First, the ideal for which we are willing to lay down our lives must be genuine, that is to say, it must be strong enough to bear the analysis of reason; secondly, there must be unflinching and uncompromising loyalty; lastly we must determine with deliberation whether the ideal can be advanced better by dying than by sensible living. It is in the second of these elements alone that the great bulk of well-meaning men are strong, in most cases ignoring entirely the third, and giving very little thought indeed to the first, if we can judge by the unanimity of patriots in any country. By being so over enthusiastic in the element of loyalty as to ignore the importance of assuring ourselves of the validity of the ideal itself, together in each case, with the best means of serving it, we have unconsciously fallen into the sentimentalism of regarding death as a virtue. We have stressed out of all proportion the element of loyalty in the ethical complex of honor. As much as we may admire the courage of a man who dies for honor, we nevertheless deplore his indifference toward his obligation to analyze the validity of the honor claims. Everything from brutal aggression to spoliation and injustice have been regarded by peoples at one time or another as obligations of honor, a fact which, if it does not prove that very little thought has been employed by those who died in its defense, must at least impute their judgment.

The foolishness of an irrational devotion to the principle of dying for "an ideal" becomes clear when we take something other than national honor. Let us suppose a man who believes in polygamy. Suppose that such a man arrived at

THE TYRANNY OF A PHRASE 145

this social ideal by as little thinking as the average man does, in assuring himself that his country's honor is at stake. Then let us suppose further that on such a weak intellectual conviction he added some inexplicable emotional assurance which when questioned he would persistently evade to answer. Suppose then that he struck out to do all in his power to spread the ideal of polygamy even at the cost of his own life. He would be criminal we would say, even though he were dying for "an ideal." Unless he spent a good many years thinking the whole marriage question out, and arrived at a definite, sincere philosophy of the marital relation, believing honestly that polygamy was the best social institution the world could adopt with regard to marriage, we would feel that he was unjustified in "acting" upon his conviction. In other words, if the ideal of polygamy just struck him as an emotional fancy, and he laid down his life for it, we could admire his courage, but hardly his ideal. Furthermore even if we granted his sincerity and maturity of conviction, we would even then in his case have to regard his dying as sheer folly, because the best thing that such a man could do for his eccentric ideal would be to live for it and spread it by every means in his power. With him would die the most ardent champion of the ideal, and it is sentiment to believe that his ideal would be advanced by martyrdom. There are many cases where death is an efficient means of advancing ideals, but the example at least shows the necessity for cool deliberation with respect to this efficiency aspect of the question of dying for an ideal.

Men hold an attitude of contempt toward compatriots who question the validity of the honor ideal, while they respect such an idealist if he happens to be a member of an enemy country. Any one in a country at war who stands out against the national honor, and questions its sacredness when men are willing to die for it on all sides, is immediately branded by his compatriots, as a coward. He is never regarded as a martyr except in rare cases, posthumously. But when a man stands out in an enemy country against the enemy national honor, he becomes straightway a martyr. To the Allies, Liebknecht is a hero and a moral giant; in Germany he is a traitor and a coward serving his sentence in jail. In Germany Bertrand Russell is a martyr; in England he is spurned and ostracized. Martyrdom assuredly is in the point of view.

By accepting a philosophy of honor which regards those who question its moral validity in any particular application, as traitors and cowards

THE TYRANNY OF A PHRASE 147

equally with those who feel that dying for a particular ideal might not help to advance it, and by insisting upon loyalty for loyalty's sake, we have come to the point of regarding death as a virtue. In their intense sincerity and earnestness, men have become blind to the obvious fact that an ideal must be reasonable, a product of the mind.

A complete rationalization of honor is necessary. We must turn a deaf ear to the majestic ring of the word as it reverberates through the emotional recesses of the mind, and attempt bravely an analysis of the bell itself as we find it in the political belfry of the twentieth century.

PART III

THREE PROGRAMS FOR
PERMANENT PEACE

CHAPTER IX

MORALIZATION OF NATIONAL HONOR.
A PROBLEM IN ETHICS

THERE is little doubt that the Peace Congress which will meet at the close of the present war, will be more ready than have been the former Conferences at the Hague, to face squarely the perplexing and delicate question of national honor. It will, we hope, make a genuine attempt to come to a more definite understandstanding of the political principles which it properly embraces in its scope, and if it is retained at all in international usage, it will be put through a thorough and exacting process of moralization. The deliberate evasion of the Second Hague Conference with regard to "vital interest and national honor" will not be repeated by a war-chastened world.

The crimes and injustices that have been committed in its name and under its sanction, are so numerous, that it is not unfair to deny to the current meaning of the term any moral significance at all. In acquiring the quality of an irresistible slogan for all wars, just and unjust alike, it is no wonder that it has lost its essential moral implication and become an empty shell; or even worse, a mockery of the very thing it professes to be.

If the nations do not agree to the arbitration of honor disputes, they will at least make a very serious effort to define it in such a way as to afford some clearly enunciated criteria by which individual cases of honor may be judged in the future. Without "some common sentiment to which the individual can make appeal,"[1] personal honor would be impossible; and in the same way a morally consistent national honor is impossible without a similar common international sentiment, not hidden in the shadowy region of emotional obscurity, but conceived in the light of reason and justice. A rationalization of honor would require a sifting of all possible honor disputes with the ultimate codification of the *approved* casus belli into an International Code of Honor accepted by the world of nations.

For this code to be of any value in preventing unrighteous wars, it would have to be based upon universal principles of justice, i.e., the ideal of honor would have to be shorn of its "impossible" accretions, and be put through a very deliberate

[1] "Dewey and Tuft"—"Ethics," p. 86.

MORALIZATION OF NATIONAL HONOR

process of moralization. None of the political philosophies by which the conduct of nations is governed to-day, could serve as a basis for this moralization. A political philosophy which might obviate conflicts of honor and still preserve justice, is not impossible. The influences which have been responsible for the degeneration and perversion of the political ideal, would, to secure moralization, have to be frankly recognized and checked; new and wholesome standards would have to be introduced into our political thinking.

If the Peace Congress attempts this task of moralization, it will not be easy. It will require more than a mere vague "uncoördinated desire for peace." Somebody will have to be entrusted to work out the implications and ramifications of such a moralization. It will necessitate the abandonment of much of our diplomatic terminology that suggest the out-worn moral confusion from which national honor must emerge. It will mean that "instinctive political morality" [1] will have to yield to law.

Let us consider briefly what such a moralization of national honor would imply; and what would be the technique as it were, by which it could be attained. It is one thing to recognize the perversions into which it has fallen; it is quite

[1] Rumelin—"Relation of Politics to Moral Law."

another to appreciate the colossal task of its remoralization.

To erect a political morality we can not build in the sands of emotion. Our first task then in the moralization process would be to assure ourselves that the new sense of honor is a rational ideal stripped of emotional accretions.

The material of morality is rational ideals, not vague æsthetic emotions; and in erecting new standards for honor we must at the outset dispel the film of emotionalism that has hitherto enveloped it.

This means first that honor will have to admit of universal application. In order to claim moral validity it will have to abandon its climatic character. The theory of an honor peculiar to each nation in the way that language or custom may be said to be peculiar, must give way to universal law. "Always act as if you would wish that action to become universal law," was Kant's admonition, and we cannot afford to overlook this in formulating an international morality. Moral law admits of no peculiar interpretations. The theory that each nation must have its own peculiar code of honor which depends upon its traditions and its "legitimate aspirations," is commonly accepted to-day. "Any one may even show," says Terraillon, "that each nation has a particular concept and a more or less clear idea of what honor means to it." This doctrine, popular as it is, could not bear moral analysis.

So long as honor is not regarded as a universal ideal but merely as the peculiar expression of each people, it is no wonder that strange inconsistencies and moral confusion arise. For example England demanded to be consulted in the drawing of the Treaty of Morocco but refused to extend this identic privilege to Germany who had the same right to it, and she defended both these positions as obligations imposed by her honor. The two citations given below illustrate this point.

"The claim that Germany made, that no treaty should be made in any part of the world without the approval of Germany was not one which a SELF-RESPECTING nation could admit." Gilbert Murray.

"If peace can only be preserved by the surrender of the great and beneficent position which Great Britain has won by centuries of heroism and achievement, by allowing England to be treated where her interests were concerned as if she were of no account in the cabinet of nations (i.e., not to be consulted in the Morocco treaty), then I say emphatically that peace at that price would be a *humiliation intolerable for a great nation like ours to endure."* Lloyd George—Mansion House Speech.

It is utter foolishness to claim ethical sanction for an ideal that works only one way.

Very important it is indeed if we wish to maintain a minimum of moral content, to provide adequate correctives for honor. If national honor is to be kept generous, we must see to it that all the influences that could keep it from demoralizing are allowed to work upon it. In the case of personal and professional honor, the correctives that insure their moralization continually, are provided for, first in the class character of it, and secondly in the freedom with which points of honor may be discussed, within the class. No deviation from the class code is tolerated until it has fought its way in against conservatism and prejudice, when it becomes generally sanctioned and assumes the same inviolable character as the other principles in the code. This has been the history of honor as it has been the history of all moral ideals. Class honor has retained its high standards through the corrective influence of associates who are quick to detect any practice which is selfish and inimical to the welfare of the group. The class character of honor has always

MORALIZATION OF NATIONAL HONOR

maintained a minimum moral level, first by defining the principles to be embodied in the code, and secondly by demanding rigorous observance of them.

Rigorous observance of the code insured moralization and an unselfish minimum. That is to say, a member was always free to improve the code, to make it even more unselfish and exacting so far as his personal conduct was concerned; but improvement could not be a peculiar interpretation which he might give to the term himself. The class determines whether the variations are indeed unselfish. It is quite conceivable, for example, that the medical profession would not condemn the practice of free service to the poor, though the ethics of the profession does not include this in the "irreducible minimum." But self-advertising would never receive anything but rigid condemnation. Physicians could erect a specious justification for advertising themselves. They might regard themselves as such skilled practitioners that it was performing a service to get themselves before the public. But the profession as a whole passes upon these matters and no individual interpretations of honor such as this would be likely to receive approval. It is to keep alive the spark of altruism that sputters in the winds of all our selfish instincts and passions, that we reserve the sacred term "honor."

Now the great difficulty with our conception of national honor is that we have transferred an ideal from the individual to the nation without providing for the corrective influences that would insure its moralization. First of all we have failed to admit in international politics that if national honor means anything at all, it must be a class ideal, and it is the family of nations which comprises that class as it is the whole community of physicians which makes it possible to talk of the honor of the medical profession, for example. So long as we renounce the class character of national honor and accept instead the theory that each nation must have its own code, it is stupid to call it "honor." We might call it "self-preservation," or the "law of national life." But if we take a term that has a very specific moral implication, remove it from its context, and then apply it to something to which it does not belong by a stretch of the most liberal interpretation, we condemn ourselves not only of stupidity but of hypocrisy.

An equivalent corrective, of course, would be some sort of a recognition by the family of nations of certain ideals of international polity with

MORALIZATION OF NATIONAL HONOR 159

respect to questions of honor. International law, however, covers only the approved practices of war, and does not provide checks against the abuse of the honor justification. *By renouncing the class character of honor among states which we accept in the case of persons, we have lost the best opportunity for the moralization of national honor, and have in our moral dilemna come to confuse the whole matter in a maze of emotional obscurity in which the unconscious forces of self-seeking and national ambition not only determine our action but color our whole thinking.*

There is another possible corrective influence which we have just as deliberately denied to national honor; namely the free and unrestrained discussion of points of honor within a nation as disputes arise. When the "custodians of the national honor" declare that "honor is at stake,"

> "Theirs not to reason why,
> Theirs but to do and die."

Any rational discussion of it is an indication to the angry Junker, not of a desire to be fair or sensible, but of cowardice and treason. Such discussion is vigorously suppressed and in this way the other possible corrective check for honor is also lost.

Consequently if we wish to restore to honor the

ethical sanction which it has lost through persistent abuse and perversion, we will have to take an entirely different attitude toward criticism from without as well as to that from within. Internal suppression of views on honor when these views happen to be unpopular, will have to be abandoned, and external criticism will have to be embraced. In this way alone can we hope to approach that ideal which must ultimately lead to an INTERNATIONAL HONOR.

Unless we consciously introduce these correctives and encourage criticism, we must sooner or later fall into the untenable position of the militarist who respects force more than justice. All the nations rigorously adhere to the principle that a national desire if it is a matter of national honor (and it is hard to discover a dispute that could not be changed into a dispute of honor) must be enforced even in defiance of the moral judgment of the world. No concert of powers, no international code, can pass judgment on the right or wrong of a question of honor. Behind the pretext of this justification, nations have taken such unwarranted stands, that the statement that "honor" (with all its vague implications), cannot be arbitrated, is a euphonious way of saying, might is right.

If instead of passing individual judgment, nations would consent to accept the judgment of an impartial world court, then unwillingness to arbitrate the disputes which this world court declared involved honor, would not indicate an adherence to the ethics of force. It might be that such a body would err, but a majority opinion of an impartial group of men trained in affairs of honor would at least be the best approximation to justice that civilization affords. It is sometimes true that the majority is wrong, and a nation that stands alone might be nearest the truth. But the chance for this is slight. The acceptance of an impartial judgment rendered by a court on affairs of honor, though it might not insure justice, at least recognizes that truth must be sought in the spirit of truth, that it is an attribute of the mind, not of the cannon.

The last step in the moralization process would demand a clear recognition that honor is an ethical complex implying the honor of two parties. Morally regarded a nation cannot dishonor another without dishonoring itself, any more than one man can hold another "in the ditch without himself remaining there." We recognize this principle in the case of individuals. A man dishonors himself in dishonoring a woman. But in the case of nations we feel that we can assert our honor independently, and do not realize that at the very best our honor is only a fractional part of the "integral moral complex" which must embrace the honor of the other side. Just as a concavity and a convexity are indispensable to a curvature, so there can be no ethical honor of one country that is coupled with a violation of the honor of another. All wars have resulted from this one-sided conception of honor.

The one-sided aberration which pervades all our political thinking in connection with the material out of which wars grow, recurs even in this purely moral question. It is true that nations do not mean to stain the honor of other countries in asserting their own, and that rationally considered they believe in the two-fold obligation which genuine honor implies. Wars of conflicting honors however would be impossible if one nation felt that the defense of its own honor was not complete without the protection of the honor of the other. If this had been the attitude of nations, then the wars of honor of the past would have to be explained as the repeated phenomena of one nation proudly defending its honor against another who persistently refuses to affront it, but whose purpose in fact is protection. We have a situation of double defense with no attack. Dr. Felix Adler in this connection says—

"The great ethical error of the world till now

has been that in righteous self-defense men have become most unrighteous, because in self-defense they have thought of their right as sundered from the right of others. Yet my right is but one blade of the shears, and the right of my fellow, even though he be the aggressor, is the other blade. . . . The employer announces his intention to crush the union of laborers, and in his blind assertion of the fractional right which is his, he destroys the integral right which is compounded of his and theirs."

Of course the reason that honor has fallen into this moral confusion and one-sidedness, is because the object of loyalty has been the nation and not humanity. To give honor genuine moral validity, "the basis of loyalty will have to be broadened," and the ideal of honor as peculiar possessions of fractional sections of humanity will have to yield to a more comprehensive ideal. By increasing the area of moral obligation we will eliminate this paradox of honor. Insistence upon a national honor has very naturally diverted men from a wider code and more fundamental general principles of morality. The serious moral objection to all codes of honor is that they are fractional, and sufficient unto themselves, bearing no relation to larger aggregates of people. The Southern patriot who owed undivided allegiance to the South and its honor, found it hard to yield to the demands of a more comprehensive national honor.

The moral world is a unit in which every act must bear a very definite relation to the whole. "The pebble that is thrown into the pond destroys the center of gravity of the universe." Every act if it is to be moral must take into account the continuity of ethical conduct. National boundaries cannot be used as legitimate barriers to interrupt this continuity.

The steps in the moralization of national honor would be, first, rationalization and universalization; secondly, the providing of adequate correctives against its demoralization, by the acceptance of external criticism and internal discussion; thirdly, the abandonment of the doctrine that each nation must be the sole judge of matters affecting its honor; fourthly, the giving up of the principle of "my country, right or wrong"; and lastly, a recognition of the two-fold implication of the honor complex. This would be a basis for the moralization of the much abused and irresistible war-slogan of national honor.

CHAPTER X

A COURT OF INTERNATIONAL HONOR.
A PROBLEM IN POLITICS

In the last chapter I outlined the ethical technique by which the moralization of national honor could be attained. In the present chapter we will consider an equally effective political scheme for accomplishing the same purpose.

It is an ethical truism that one country's national honor will approach perfect moralization only in so far as it takes into account the just demands of other countries. Excessive and unjust requirements must be modified to meet the legitimate aspirations of other nations, if any particular code of national honor is to become moral.

Now in order to make these ethical adjustments with regard to foreign policies one thing is imperative. It is necessary that all the nations enunciate very definitely and clearly their respective codes of honor, declaring in unequivocal terms those elements of foreign policy which if disputed would involve national honor. Without such diplomatic candor nothing can be accomplished.

To facilitate the articulation and the later adjustment of separate honor policies, A COURT OF INTERNATIONAL HONOR must be created in which all the distinct national obligations of honor will be considered and compared. To formulate a code of honor which will embrace for each nation all the important elements of foreign policy that might be said to involve honor, will, it is true, be a colossal and embarrassing task. The vague character of "honor," the ease with which it may be involved in almost any dispute, and the elusive way in which it escapes definition, would make the function of the court "delicate" indeed. But more than this, its function would be impeded by the fact that nations would very reluctantly remove their honor skeletons from the diplomatic closets to expose them to the scorn of an international public opinion. It is quite possible for a nation to accept silently in time of peace a specious foreign policy, and were it disputed, to rise deluded by passion and proclaim it a matter of national honor to defend it; it is quite another thing for a nation to declare in a time of dispassionate calm, before a world tribunal, that it proposed to adhere as an obligation of honor to a policy which was obviously one of questionable character. A nation preserves its sense of justice as well as its sense of humor much better in times of peace than in a moment of impending war.

The COURT OF INTERNATIONAL HONOR would not necessarily be a Court of Arbitration. Its task of defining, codifying and amending the separate national codes of honor in accordance with the political, economic and social demands and aspirations of the respective nations, would more than justify its existence. It is to be expected that the problem of defining in any adequate way the obligations imposed by a nation's honor upon its foreign policies, will be a delicate thing, and it will in many cases help matters to define the codes by a process of definite exclusion of certain matters as those not involving honor, as well as by inclusion.

Let us suppose such a Court to exist. What would be the ease with which a given dispute, apparently involving economics or politics, could be converted into an affair of honor. Let us suppose further, that England had incorporated into her code of honor which was on record at the Court, that she would never regard a boundary dispute as an affair involving her honor. And suppose that the Venezuelan boundary dispute should come up again. Any complications of such a dispute that might arise because of offensive attitudes or abusive language would be the only possible "honor" ground on which the two nations might clash. But no nation would really go to war because of a mere attitude or a slighting phrase used by one diplomat to another. The court then would be asked to determine whether the dispute was a boundary matter without "complications." England would not be compelled to abide by the decision, but at least she would have the clearly articulated judgment of an authoritative Court that the dispute involved a question of boundary and nothing else, and that if she went to war about it, it would be in violation of her pledge as embodied in her code of honor.

This purely judicial function of determining whether a given dispute falls under one of the articulated categories of the respective national codes of honor bears no relation at all to the question of arbitrating these disputes. When Congress passes an Anti-Trust Law defining a trust as a monopoly in restraint of trade and the Supreme Court is called in to decide whether or not a certain practice or combination is in restraint of trade, we have not delegated to the Supreme Court the power to pass Anti-Trust legislation.

The effect of articulating and codifying the respective codes of honor would be twofold. A frank analysis of the whole problem in the task of defining and collating, would bring to the surface all sorts of hidden and obscure sources of conflict which would not bear up under reason and the moral pressure of an organized Court. Definite codification in the INTERNATIONAL COURT OF HONOR would have the effect of stripping the honor sentiment of its pettiness, its foolishness, and its morbid "touchiness." The vague concept in the case of each nation would be rationalized into a definite body of honor demands which could not be generalized, emotionalized, or stretched in their meaning and application. The existence of a definite code and a Court of Honor would be a very effective "restraining influence" on the excesses of the honor justification.

A similar court of honor was instituted in the days of chivalry and dueling, and its effect was to rationalize the whole conception on generally accepted ideals. The air was cleared of emotion and passion and definite rational standards replaced nondescript moral emotions, which, just as they had no definite character in themselves, needed no definite stimuli to arouse them. A codification of national honors done in the light of an international public opinion would result in establishing the sentiment upon a universal interpretation of right and justice, and would create an atmosphere which would make adjustment and moralization possible. Without knowing very accurately the data which we wish to rationalize and adjust to broader principles of humanity, it would indeed be difficult to make any progress. Our first step in moralization is to know the raw material, the things to be moralized; and here codification of clearly articulated policies would be imperative.

In addition to paving the way for moralization, a codification of national honors would bring to light all the potential honor conflicts. Such a process would not be anticipating wars which might otherwise rest, potentially smoldering, because there would arise altogether too many conflicts involving one nation after another, for war to appear in any way attractive or sensible for the settling of these disputes. The United States for example might clash with nearly the whole world on the Monroe Doctrine, with Japan on the question of immigration, with Canada on tariff arrangements, with Japan again with regard to the Philippines, involving perhaps every other nation on the globe. With such an array of possible honor disputes for the United States to settle, we would refrain from declaring war against the entire world. When the enemy is a single nation and when the offense is a single offense clearly perceived, the chance for war is great; but when the offenses are only potential, when they are numerous, and when they involve almost every other nation, the situation is quite different. Since disagreements would all of them be merely academic, and brought about not in the course of an actual clash, but simply as a result of an honest desire to remove and adjust the potential causes of friction, it is very likely that a certain amount of judicial calm would envelop the disputes. To say that there would be a great world conflagration anticipated, is to overlook the scale upon which such a war would have to be repeated and repeated. The alignment of enemy and friend would be so complicated that war would be impossible and highly unreasonable. With the interplay, and overlapping of economic, political and social interests, generally, no nation would be a clear-cut and absolute enemy to any other nation, and every nation would probably be in some measure an enemy to all other nations. *With a clear declaration of honor policies and their resulting conflicts, there would be such complicated disagreements, oppositions and alignments, each nation being the center of a rapid fire of criticism of its articulated honor policies that there would be engendered as the only alter-*

native to perpetual world war, a candid desire to adjust these manifold disagreements. All phases of the diplomatic negotiations, it is safe to say, as a result of the present war, will be followed by an intelligent and enlightened public interest which will help to clear the atmosphere of greed and unreasonableness. In the fire of an international public opinion working on the whole honor problem, national honor will be divorced from national advantage.

In the great kaleidoscopic jumble of potential honor conflicts which the codification would give rise to in the International Court, the alignments of national interests would criss-cross in so many ways that where with respect to the Bagdad railway, for example, England would be an enemy to Germany, she would be a friend to her with respect to their common opposition to the Monroe Doctrine. It is not reasonable to suppose that England, in view of this paradoxical relation of friendship and enmity, would first fight against Germany on account of her ambition for an opening into the East, then turn around and ally herself with Germany to fight America because of common antagonism to the Monroe Doctrine. France would be with Belgium in the matter of her inviolable neutrality but against her with respect to the Belgian Congo. This does not mean that she would both fight and protect Belgium. And so we would find if all policies were clearly enunciated, that each nation would in one or more respects be a friend as well as a potential enemy to every other nation.

This great confusion would of itself convince rulers and diplomats of the sheer madness of casting their choice for war as a means of settlement. It would place each nation in the impossible condition of expecting the support of a country with respect to an honor policy with which that country sympathized, on the one hand, and on the other hand, seeking to defeat by war the same country because of its opposition to another honor policy. But perhaps the greatest effect of the Court of International Honor would be felt in the public education which would follow as a result of the destruction of secret diplomacy and the consequent exposure of the unworthiness of many national honor policies of every country, followed by the awakening realization of the utter stupidity of resorting to war as a means of settling these bewilderingly numerous and totally unreasonable diplomatic claims. When this clearing process begins, when people are ready to abandon the ideal of "my country right or wrong," we will have made the greatest step in internationalization that has yet been achieved.

The codes that are compiled will of course have to be painfully specific and definite. As time goes on each nation will want to modify and amend its honor policies. However difficult this may be, the situation will have to be accepted, for the code must not be allowed to fall behind the time, become indefinite or obscure, general or ambiguous. Uncompromising rigidity and exacting definiteness would be its only excuse for being.

The effect of clear declaration of policy can not be overestimated. Let us suppose that England had definitely stated in unequivocal terms and had registered its attitude with the Court, to wit: "That England will regard it as a matter of national honor to use all its military and economic forces to prevent and to repel an invasion of Belgium." Let us further suppose that all the signatories to the treaty which guaranteed Belgian neutrality had stated just as clearly their position and recorded these honor obligations with the Court Is it likely that in the face of bringing down upon herself universal condemnation through a violation of the honor obligations of the civilized world, Germany would have dared

A COURT OF INTERNATIONAL HONOR 175

to invade Belgium? It is said that if England's attitude alone had been clearly perceived, if Germany had been sure that England's honor was genuinely bound up with Belgian neutrality, it is very doubtful whether she would have gone to war.

Declaration of honor policies would clear the international skies from all the overhanging clouds of suspicion and fear, and would eliminate secret diplomacy and national subterfuge, hidden undercurrents of policy, and all the other material out of which wars arise.

Who can say how many wars have been averted through the clear and definite articulation of the Monroe Doctrine for example? The very clarity with which the doctrine is couched, has served to ward off possible opposition to it which nations might have felt in the dim regions of subconscious antagonism. Our position is so clearly understood that an offense to our honor in that particular could not hide behind any veil of misunderstanding, fear or suspicion. It would be clearly an insult to our honor not unconsciously, but because of the definiteness of the Doctrine, deliberately inflicted. Nations rarely oppose a clearly enunciated policy, but fight more effectively when the purpose of a war is vague, elastic and indefinite. It is something of the psy-

176 WHAT IS "NATIONAL HONOR"?

chology of wonder which makes wars successful. If the real causes of wars which usually come out specifically in the terms of peace, were blazoned before the people before the wars, it is doubtful whether such an atmosphere of candor would add zest to the patriot. Confusion, vagueness, generalities, and the indefinite irresistible slogan of national honor, are the very air which the war spirit breathes.

The value of definiteness and codification of honor principles and policies lies of course chiefly in that they would remove the temptation to emotionalize the issue. Stripped of its vague emotional accretions and boldly defined, a dispute of honor will lose its irresistible glamor which inheres more than in anything else in its very indefiniteness, and it will become a legal or judicial question relatively easy to settle. Wolff, in his suggestive work on "International Government," cites an interesting example of the effect of rational preventives on the matter of devitalizing the emotional possiblities of an honor dispute.

"There will never be a case in which national honor is more dangerously and vitally affected than it was in the Dogger Bank incident. The danger lay in the fact that the honor of the Russian fleet was in question when Lord Lansdowne demanded apology. . . . War as usual in such

A COURT OF INTERNATIONAL HONOR 177

cases appeared inevitable. . . . But it so happened that there had been invented at the first Hague Conference a Procedure of International Inquiry which enabled the Dogger Bank question to be put to a Tribunal in a judicial form. A difference involving honor was therefore reduced to the common legal and judicial question of fact and of the degree of responsibility and blame attaching to the different persons for the results of certain actions. And so the inevitable war was avoided."

Another very important constructive thing could be done with the welter of conflicting national honor demands which the Court would have at its disposal. The Court of International Honor would be a Clearing House which would deal in national honor securities and consequently be in a fair position to pass on the solvency, the moral validity of the separate securities in the light of broader principles of justice and humanity. Out of this great mass of honor policies some will recommend themselves as genuine while others will condemn themselves as spurious. The Court might not have the power to compel a nation to withdraw its insistence upon some policy which it did not approve. But it is not overoptimistic to hope that such a Court might be invested with the power of recommendation.

The constructive work of the Court of International Honor, then, would be to examine and collate certain honor policies of the separate nations, which it approved; to incorporate them into a Code of International Honor; to put the moral force and if possible the military force of a League to Enforce Peace, behind these accepted policies. Such a code would be the only sustaining sentiment for any international police force that might be created after the war, and the advantage of the codification of this sentiment of honor in its various aspects, would be to make the function of the international force clear and definite. The result would be not only that it would know exactly what to do, but that the separate nations would know clearly and in advance what not to do, which so far as securing peace is concerned is a great deal more important.

Of course what would be incorporated into this international code of honor would be only the generous national honor policies, to which would be added generally accepted practices of international law. For example, America's protectorate over Cuba might very probably be approved by a majority vote of the Court, and be incorporated into the new international code behind which would be placed all the military and moral power

A COURT OF INTERNATIONAL HONOR 179

of the nations. England's policy in New Zealand, America's attitude toward the Panama Canal, France in Morocco, and other definite and more or less approved policies would be specifically embodied with the result that it would not only strengthen these accepted policies, but by contrast would lend a moral weakness and nakedness to these excluded policies, even though the court did not have the power to condemn and eliminate the more selfish practices of individual national honors. The silent condemnation which in effect exclusion from an international code of honor would mean, might work wonders.

The plan of codification together with an organized force behind the code is not Utopian. Such a staunch nationalist as Ex-President Roosevelt endorses some such scheme.

"My proposal is that the efficient civilized nations—those that are efficient in war as well as in peace—shall join in a world League for the peace of righteousness.— This means that they shall by solemn covenant agree as to their respective rights which shall not be questioned; that they shall agree that all other questions arising between them shall be submitted to a Court of Arbitration."

But the new world League to Enforce Peace will not be able to proceed on the basis of a mere pooling of selfish national aims. Each one of these aims will have to stand the test of international validity. Such validity will be determined by an international public opinion influencing the Court and its work. The trouble with international public opinion heretofore has been that it was not organized; that there was no official body through which it could express itself, so that any moral pressure which it would unquestionably have been able to exert if it had been organized and articulated, has been lost. Wells correctly says, that "the trouble with the peace movement is that there is no authoritative body whose business it is to see that peace is maintained." Nor is it any one's business to crystallize international public opinion for a nation about to enter war. Of course a nation can get snatches of foreign sentiment from the press of foreign countries, and from other public utterances; but it does not really know the attitude that other nations as a whole feel toward it in a dispute in which it is about to engage. The situation is aggravated by the desire which nations feel to be neutral, as a result of which that spontaneous judgment is crushed, which if it were enunciated would help to create the strongest possible instrument for fair play and humanity. A dignified expression of world opinion upon

A COURT OF INTERNATIONAL HONOR 181

every dispute that arose between nations, would compel the nation in the wrong to withdraw, or if not to withdraw at least to lose heart, while it would strengthen the side that was declared to be right. No nation in its senses would willingly disregard the officially articulated judgment of the nations, to stand condemned by a world court of honor, and to reveal itself in the moral nakedness of an outlaw among nations. When the stakes were large it might be that moral pressure would be ineffective; but when the issues involved were less vital, a sense of national humor would supplant an unreasoning sense of national honor and peaceable adjustment would result. MacFarland has this to say of the power of moral pressure—

"At once and in a word I am still one of those who believe that international public opinion is the power and the only power which can produce compliance with the award of an international tribunal, whether that be an international arbitration tribunal or a judicial tribunal as a world court."

Whatever means are used to enforce a judgment of the court, whether it be the military power of a society of nations, economic pressure, isolation, or the combined moral pressure of international public opinion alone, the important thing is to have the judgment articulated in every great crisis which might be seen to be leading to war. The Court will not be able to control national honor policies directly, but its indirect effect would be tremendous, and in so far as policies of aggression were concerned, no nation would dare to violate international honor in such a flagrant way. Elihu Root says in this connection:

"Law cannot control national policy, and it is through the working of long continued and persistent national policies that the present war has come. Against such policies all attempts at conciliation and understanding and good will among nations of Europe have been powerless. But law if enforced can control the external steps by which a nation seeks to follow a policy, and rules may be so framed that a policy of aggression cannot be worked out except through open violations of law which will meet the protest and condemnation of the world at large backed by whatever means shall have been devised for law enforcement."

The fear that the moral pressure of a well-defined international judgment will not be adequate, is unfounded. It is said that since the re-entry of arbitration into the world with the Jay Treaty, there has not been a single important case of a refusal to abide by a judgment. Na-

A COURT OF INTERNATIONAL HONOR 183

tions have often refused to submit disputes to arbitration, but when they have actually agreed to arbitrate, "they have invariably abided by the tribunal of their own choice." In 1891 judgment had been given against Venezuela in favor of Peru which the former refused to abide by. But such cases are rare.

The proposed International Court of Honor then, would formulate an international morality of casus belli, adopted and sanctioned by a Congress of powers as "honorable" policies, upheld by an international sentiment of honor, and, if possible, defended by the physical power of a League to Enforce Peace. Enough time has been devoted to giving an international sanction to the rules of war. After all it is not such a vital thing in the interests of peace to have a body of conventions which recognize certain methods of killing as preferable and more civilized than others. A genuine peace tribunal would consider the means of securing peace rather than a method of humanizing war. What would we think of a state where there were no laws against murder, but very explicit and detailed laws governing proper methods of murder? The psychological effect of such laws would be to encourage murder and crime by the very recognition of them in law, even if that recognition consisted only in a most vigorous disapproval. A description of legitimate and approved violence has no ethical prohibition per se.

In the place of the international honor and morality which the two Hague Conferences codified, and in which war was taken for granted and merely humanized, our Court of International Honor would establish an international morality of peace, a clearly enunciated and codified sentiment of international honor, which would recognize peace as the normal and proper relation among states. Aside from the profound moral and psychological effect which this shift of emphasis would have, its practical constructive influence on maintaining peace would be tremendous.

The first chapter in the code of international honor of course would be to recognize the Court's authority, to respect its recommendations, and to abide by its judgments. It will do little good to have a police force to enforce judgments if our new INTERNATIONAL HONOR does not accept as its first obligation, the principle of abiding and accepting the Court's judgments. Each nation must not be allowed further to build up its own military strength, or we might easily have another war like the present, in which the forces

A COURT OF INTERNATIONAL HONOR 185

of the world were arraigned against the military power of a recalcitrant group.

Too much time must not be spent as was true at the second Hague Conference, in defining the rights of neutrals. The "rights of neutrals" important though they are, presuppose war and hence cannot be said to be a step in the direction of peace. The lack of enthusiasm with which nations have backed such conventions shows its appeal as an instrument of peace. It is no wonder that an international honor which merely recognized certain approved methods of war did not rouse the enthusiasm of nations. If Russia and Japan should happen to be at war and Japan should violate the neutrality of French Indo-China, it is not likely that the world would throw itself into a paroxysm of offended honor. There is nothing in such an abstract violation to stir the emotions, and without emotions the psychic recognition of an offense, as I have shown elsewhere, is cold and colorless. A great deal more enthusiasm could be aroused for constructive ideals of peace, justice and humanity, if these things were codified into INTERNATIONAL HONOR, than has been aroused by violations of abstract principles of international law defining the rules of civilized barbarity.

There is little question that with regard to the rules that the two Hague Conferences laid down as the laws of war, no real sense of INTERNATIONAL HONOR exists. This is not because nations do not intellectually approve of the Hague Conventions. In times of peace no nation ever questions them. It is only in time of war when the intellectual approval finds it difficult to hold its own against the battering force of emotional necessity, that compromise is inevitable even with the most enlightened nations. How can we talk of the existence to-day of a sense of international honor with regard to the rights of neutrals for example to which at the second Hague Conference all the nations were signatories, when we have such a contradiction as this: "On the one hand we have a treaty most solemnly guaranteeing the inviolability or the permanent neutrality of a country like Belgium let us say, and on the other hand the conviction on the part of the government of that country that it would not be justified in diminishing its army by one single soldier on the strength of this guarantee."

The problem of the future will be to create a sense of international honor that is not pale and divorced from emotion, but fervent and militant; a sense of international honor which will not merely feel offended at open violations of peace

A COURT OF INTERNATIONAL HONOR

and the laws of peace, and the refusal of a nation to abide by the judgment of the Court, but an emotional sense of international honor that will be just as passionate, just as virile and just as genuine as national honor is to-day. Passionate nationalism must be enlarged not to academic internationalism, but to a real throbbing sense of emotional international honor.

"Only when the great nations of the world have reached some sort of an agreement," says President Wilson, "as to what they hold to be fundamental to their common interests, and to some feasible method of acting in concert when any nation or group of nations seeks to disturb those fundamental things, can we feel that civilization is at last in a way of justifying its existence."

The ways and means of fusing the vital human force of emotion with the cold abstraction of international honor, which is to be the slogan of the new era, will be considered in the next chapter.

CHAPTER XI

AN EMOTIONAL EQUIVALENT FOR NATIONAL HONOR.

A PROBLEM IN PSYCHOLOGY

The emotional values which are inseparably associated with national honor are for the most part not only æsthetic but indispensable to a normal expression of human nature. It would be impossible to crush the perfectly natural love for these values without destroying the source of much that is good and beautiful in men's character. Our problem is either to change the impulses, or re-shape the end which they serve. Human nature in its basic instincts is unchanging; national honor which has hitherto been the medium through which all the dramatic impulses have found collective expression, is not on the other hand, an absolute unalterable ideal. Of the two human nature then must be accepted as it is; the dramatic impulses however may be directed along lines of constructive good toward something broader and deeper than merely "national" honor. *In other words we must find for national honor, which has up to the present been the sole incentive for the dramatic mass tendencies of men, an emotional equivalent.*

It is altogether human for every man occasionally to indulge in violent dislike. It makes little difference whether the object of the animosity happens to be Mexico, or capital or woman suffrage, or the Oshkosh *Gazette,* provided only our natural disposition to rant, is satisfied. Vehement hatred is an intense dramatic value especially when it carries with it all the mass momentum of a great and powerful nation. Now then, we can either condemn the human trait which seeks an emotional joy in hatred, or we can find some other more desirable objective for this passion.

In a similar way men love a good fight with all the dramatic possibilities of success and failure. The spectacle of nations in battle is the arch drama of civilization, shot through with almost every possible human emotional appeal. Here too we can either check pugnacity, or change the end, by resetting the scenes of international politics; we can either suppress the impulse to fight, or again, find a more reasonable objective for its activity. Other emotional values can be cited. Our problem then is to provide for all the emotional values which inhere in an expression of national honor, a composite emotional equivalent.

The basic cause for war is the impulses which find to-day in national honor alone a field for expression. *Our object should be to direct these impulses into a sentiment of international honor which offers a dramatic and æsthetic setting within which they could express just as effectively, and provides that emotional equivalent that not only does no violence to human nature, but ministers to it as perfectly as does the ideal of national honor.* The dramatic tendencies would find in INTERNATIONAL HONOR not only an enlarged stage for creative activity, but a very much enlarged audience, unanimously sympathetic, which circumstance would lend additional dramatic force to any emotion that might be felt. By creating a sentiment of international honor in a world federation, national honor would gradually disappear, just as aggressive state honor ceased to exist when the United States was confederated, even though state loyalties had been passionately strong, and interstate hatreds and antagonisms equally violent. Every step in federation, and federation has been the history of progress, has involved a sacrifice of the smaller honor to the more comprehensive one. We are now ready to take the last step in increasing the

AN EMOTIONAL EQUIVALENT 191

moral area of honor, and, in fact, integrating it, so that its ethical inhibitions will no longer stop at the frontier. And in order to do this we must bring into being a new arena of conflict, similar to that of national honor in dramatic possibilities, yet broader in its basic loyalties, and operating under more comprehensive principles of justice and right. This would supply an emotional equivalent for the emotions underlying national honor which so long as human nature remains as it is, must be retained, while it would obviate the moral shortcomings and the destructive quality of national honor. Such an equivalent would do away with war, at least in the intensely national spirit in which it exists to-day. It would furthermore internationalize military power in the best interests of humanity. To hope for a world without some use of force is to indulge in a Utopian dream. To think of a world without some ideal of honor likewise, for which men, when they are roused to a passionately unselfish idealism, can lay down their lives, is to overlook what may be called the emotional imperative of human nature.

If we are to retain an emotional balance in our transition from national to international honor, we must keep all the dramatic and æsthetic stage setting and associations of national honor. Unless we make the international sentiment a real emotional equivalent, this new sentiment will not be imbued with the same actuating power as the thing out of which it must evolve. We must be careful to preserve all the outward forms which have supplied so many vital emotional stimuli in the complex of national honor, and attain the new sentiment by changing only the substance. The dramatic figure of the soldier whose daring and strength have become emotionally intrenched in human nature through untold expressions of eulogy in song, verse, novels, drama, sculpture and oratory through the ages, the soldier's part must continue to be the title rôle in our new international drama. But the horizon of his purpose must be broadened. The gun with its tragic power of life and death cannot be discarded in our new setting; but its thunder must proclaim a new note of high resolve. The flag must continue to stream in the breeze against the picturesque dawn, but this time a flag of new design. And if any international symbol is to be inspiring, it will have to be as Percy Mackaye suggests, something more dramatic "than the meek symbol of a dove which the artless disciples of peace present." To destroy the emotional and moral ideal of loyalty would be to kill the root of the moral life; we must however "broaden its basis."

AN EMOTIONAL EQUIVALENT 193

Force must not be eliminated but internationalized; valor not condemned but sensibly applied. In other words honor, the slogan which opens up an arena of passionate conflict, with its spectacular display of æsthetic emotions in mass setting must be preserved; but the objective of honor can be changed from national to international. The basis for the activity of honor can be enlarged but the honor instinct can not be stamped out. We can increase the area of moral obligation but we cannot rule the ideal of obligation out of men's consciences by any impractical scheme of reform.

To say that the basis of the honor obligation cannot be broadened without doing violence to the dramatic side, and the emotional value of its expression, is to contradict the testimony of history. Honor is a class ideal, the ideal of a fragment of humanity, the object of its loyalty always being a group, a professional class, a national unit. As these units increased and became more comprehensive, the honor obligation naturally kept pace to coincide always with the new grouping, for obviously conflicting honor loyalties were never countenanced by any unit. And the history of federation proves one thing very clearly, namely, that the social and political basis of honor is not a constant factor, and that while its essential nature is unchanging, the objects of its loyalty change with the vicissitudes of politics and social organization. During the middle ages, for example, national honor in the sense of loyalty to a political group was submerged by what might be termed religious honor, the latter loyalty crossing political frontiers and disintegrating political units. On the other hand apparently incompatible social and religious units have made common national honor, as, for example, the cases of Austria and Switzerland. In other words, the form of honor, that is loyalty to some definite class, whether the cohesive bond be a political, religious or social ideal, has always been a constant, while the content, that is the size or character of the groups, admits readily of variation. Honor being a class ideal, it follows that the moment such a class is embraced by a more comprehensive group the particular class honor disappears. When the separate states of America federated into the American Union, the class "states" ceased to be a moral absolute, and consequently the code of honor that characterized states as distinct moral entities became an anachronism. In the same way the creation of a federated league of nations, if the proper emotional associations were established around the honor expression of such a league, would destroy the class

AN EMOTIONAL EQUIVALENT

"nation" as an aggressive political unit, and national honor which rests upon the theory that the nation is a moral absolute, would be modified, and gradually disappear as its place was taken by the larger honor loyalty.

Now the problem for pacifists is to create inductively this new sentiment of international honor. A world federation of course would be imperative as the first step in this direction; but federation, mechanical and impersonal, would not give rise automatically to a genuine sentiment. It is quite possible to think of a very effective political federation of nations which would break up into national states again in time of stress if the sentiment to sustain federation were lacking. On the other hand if the sentiment really existed, the external political machinery of federation would be but a mere form. We have many laws on the statute books, our "blue laws" for example, which are not real or effective because public opinion is not back of them. The spirit of law may easily have a very real existence without the letter, but it does not work so easily the other way. And so no objective political arrangement of nations per se will attain our purpose, without the sustaining emotional equivalent. An academic international honor might be said to exist to-day in the so-called family of nations, but

196   WHAT IS "NATIONAL HONOR"?

it is not a dynamic force in world politics. World organization cannot be depended upon to provide anything but a very fragile outline; for the real substance of the new honor we must look elsewhere.

We will not find the substance for our new sentiment in "education" and intellectual propaganda along the lines of internationalism. If there is one thing the present war eminently proves, it is that education toward world peace has not been effective. Intellectual appeals for peace do not seem to register. Men go to war fully conscious of its stupidity, of its horror, of its economic illusions, of its moral degradation. *To stop war we must substitute for the emotions that sustain it, counter emotions that are stronger, not intellectual subtleties about the legal, political, or economic advantages of internationalism.* We must administer the psychological treatment of creating opposite and stronger sentiments for the ones we wish to eliminate. Emotional habits like physical habits are influenced less by reasoning than by a sort of counter irritation.

Instead of creating an "international mind," we will have to mold the INTERNATIONAL HEART, *if we wish to make real the dream of a sentiment of* INTERNATIONAL HONOR. *Instead of learning*

AN EMOTIONAL EQUIVALENT

to THINK *internationally we must learn to* FEEL *internationally. Rationally in time of peace most men "distrust profoundly the common meaning of the term national honor" and approve some sort of morality which does not stop at the border line, but in time of war the situation reverts again to a sort of emotional determinism. National honor is again invested with emotional validity that with respect to its dynamic power to determine action surpasses all conceivable rational incentives. We cannot afford to discount this experience which has been only too often driven home to us when we have felt intellectually so ready for the dawn of that new era of permanent peace. We must recognize the simple truth that our intellectual honor will never be* THOUGHT, *but* "FELT" *into existence.*

The fact that we recognize national honor to be an emotional structure does not mean that the objective of it may not and should not admit of rationalization. Such a process would be especially imperative in the creation of our new sentiment of international honor. In fact the more exacting and definite that rationalization, the more steady would be the frame-work of the whole new sentiment. But things could not stop at that point. While the objective must be rationalized and broadened from national to international, the honor complex proper must be carried over. Into the new rational frame-work must be poured the emotional content which is the dynamic power of the whole in the case of national honor. Statesmen and intellectuals may *think* international honor with a fine discrimination and clarity, but if we wish to insure the support of nations as mass units, it is necessary that "the man in the streets" be made to *feel* the sentiment with the same heart glow with which he senses the national honor sentiment at present. Unless the emotional content is preserved intact and is merely transferred to the newer ideal of international honor, it is useless to hope that it may ever become an effective and vital equivalent. We know that martyrs who will die for a conviction are rare, but soldiers and patriots who will give their lives for a series of emotional satisfactions, are the most common thing in the world. In organizing a clientele for the sentiment of international honor therefore, we must enlist every device of psychology to catch and appeal to this side of human nature. We must recognize the fact that there are millions of men who would gladly go to war even for peace, because the irrefutable argument that peace can be secured in that way, has entered them via the emotions, but they would be slow to give a dollar to the Carnegie Endowment for International Peace when their persuasion that the Association is serving the same end has merely been intellectual.

I maintain therefore that in persuading the man in the streets of the validity and idealism of a sentiment of international honor, our public forum must be the heart rather than the mind, and by changing our pacifist tactics in this essential alone can we hope to succeed in the creation of the GREAT INTERNATIONAL EMOTION which would be the only abiding and unfaltering guarantee for the peace of the future.

This change in our modus operandi means that we will have to abandon the profound academic discussions and expositions of the merits of internationalism, all that abstract argument for peace which persuades, and perhaps only temporarily, only those who are already persuaded, and does not reach the great "voiceless masses" who do the fighting. I do not mean that the average man does not agree that peace is to be preferred to war, but of what avail is a mild intellectual opposition to war, when the heart cries "come." Intellectual appeals do not reach the mass, and persuade even "intellectuals" only until the next war approaches, when all the mental checks are swept to one side.

Pacifists, more than any group of reformers,

have committed what psychologists call the "intellectualist fallacy." Every pacifist *argues* the merits of peace. The American Association for International Conciliation is a representative peace society, and its tactics are those of the peace organizations the world over. For more than ten years it has been rationally educating the world for peace by putting the leading "jurists and economists of the world at work in the service of humanity to ascertain just what have been and are THE LEGAL AND ECONOMIC INCIDENTS OF WAR, AND JUST WHAT ARE THE LEGAL AND ECONOMIC ADVANTAGES TO FOLLOW UPON THE ORGANIZATION OF THE WORLD INTO A SINGLE GROUP OF FRIENDLY AND COÖPERATING NATIONS BOUND TOGETHER BY THE TIE OF A JUDICIAL SYSTEM RESTING UPON THE MORAL CONSCIOUSNESS OF MANKIND."

This has been the program in general of all pacifist propaganda. It is based upon the erroneous assumption that the underlying reason for war, in fact the "only remaining obstacle to peace," is that men believe in the economic and other advantages of the military system, and that once this intellectual prop has been removed, men will no longer see any sense in fighting. This false view that men fight out of a finely calculated economic hedonism, out of intellectual persuasion of the advantages of war, has been the

AN EMOTIONAL EQUIVALENT 201

Achilles tendon of all pacifist technique. As I tried to show in my first chapter, the remote and vaguely perceived causes of war may be economic, or the ex-post-facto justification for it, may be that certain benefits are incidental to war; but the great underlying current upon which these intellectual perceptions float as mere bubbles which burst in their impotence to modify the current into spray that is swept along, the underlying motives which actuate nations as nations to fight, is that structure of emotional imperatives in human nature which finds in war its most satisfying objectives. If then peace advocates are to destroy the fundamental cause of war they must direct their efforts to emotional persuasion, to the task of providing an emotional equivalent for the buoyant emotions upon which war rests.

I do not mean to say that leading pacifists do not themselves admit the weakness of intellectual persuasion for peace, but they have not acted absolutely upon their recognition of this. Dr. Nicholas Murray Butler, for example, admits that "it is astonishing how even men of the highest intelligence and the largest responsibility will be swept off their feet in regard to international matters at some moment of strong national feeling or on the occasion of some incident which appeals powerfully to the sentiments or the passions of the people. At the very moment when the nation most needs the guidance of its sober-minded leaders of opinion, that guidance is likely to be found wanting. . . . One who wishes to know how difficult it is to acquire the international mind in the presence of a great wave of national feeling has only to read this important paper by Mr. Adams" (on the Trent Affair).

An interesting illustration of the failure of the "intellectualist pacifism" appeared in one of our foremost magazines. Several years ago Norman Angell wrote his epoch making work—"The Great Illusion," which was generally accepted by economists all over the world. In speaking of Alsace-Lorraine Mr. Angell maintained that, "the whole notion of national possession benefiting the individual is founded upon mystification, upon an illusion. Germany conquered France and annexed Alsace-Lorraine. The "Germans" consequently "own" it and enrich themselves with the newly acquired wealth. That is my critic's view as it is the view of most European statesmen; and it is all false. Alsace-Lorraine IS OWNED BY ITS INHABITANTS AND NOBODY ELSE; AND GERMANY WITH ALL HER RUTHLESSNESS HAS NOT BEEN ABLE TO DISPOSSESS THEM. . . . Prussia the conqueror pays just as much and no less than Alsace the conquered who, if she were not paying this $5,600,000 (taxes) to Germany, would be paying it, or according to my critic a much larger sum to France; and if Germany did not own Alsace-Lorraine she would be relieved of charges that amount not to five but many more millions. The change of ownership does not therefore of itself change the money position of either owner or owned. . . . Thus we realize that when Germany has 'captured' Alsace-Lorraine she has captured a province worth 'cash value' in my critic's phrase, $330,000,000. What we overlook is that Germany has also captured the people who own the property and who continue to own it. We have multiplied by X but we have overlooked the fact that we have had to divide by X."

This economic truism seemed so obvious that political economists were literally ashamed of themselves for not having seen it before. And yet to-day such an eminent publicist as Stephen Brooks propounds the illusion all over again. In an article in the *North American Review* he insists—

"The soil of the lost provinces has made Germany's fortunes. She has derived from it her metallurgical ascendancy, the motive power for her industries, HER WEALTH, and as a consequence her moral, military and political power." ... "In the fate of Alsace-Lorraine there is involved nothing less than the industrial primacy of Europe."

This position is the more absurd when we realize that in the last 40 years while the ore deposits were in the "possession" of Germany, it was a protective tariff imposed upon the importation of iron from Alsace by the French government itself, which kept the ore from flowing into France which it would have done to the extent that Frenchmen were willing to pay as much or more for the ore than Germans.

The plan of abstract education as to the advantages of peace and the illusion of war, has evidently proved ineffective. By persuading our minds for peace we are rolling the stone of Sisyphus which, after we have painfully rolled it almost to the summit of the hill, suddenly breaks from our grasp as we become aware of a great emotional upheaval; we turn about heart-broken only to follow the rock as it tears down and crashes to the bottom again.

The future of the peace problem rests in the creation of the INTERNATIONAL HEART. This is not a plea for emotionalism in our much vaunted rational twentieth century, but a candid recognition of human nature as it is, and of the fact that the cause of internationalism therefore will never be realized until this simple truth has been taken into account in shaping our peace propaganda. What good is it to know that "sober-minded" men are always swept off their feet by emotion in time of crisis, if we dismiss this phenomenon and proceed to pile up more arguments to "educate" more thoroughly these sober minds? Is it that they may surprise us even more at the next crisis? Knowing this it seems that we might sensibly change our modus operandi instead of persisting in propaganda which, we are continually being reminded, is useless.

We must utilize the wonderfully powerful emotional force that at present exists for war, in the interests of peace by re-setting the emotional associations in connection with which this unreasoning force evolves. When we have accomplished this, then all the argument in the world will not avail to persuade us of the benefits of war. When this change of heart takes place we can then imagine the reverse situation becoming common, namely, a nation although persuaded intellectually of the economic or other disadvantages of a certain military course being suddenly swept off its feet for peace by the compelling force of the emotional complex of international honor.

Now the technique by which a sentiment of international honor can be created must be the same as that which created the sentiment of national honor. All of its characteristics will be the same except that the geographical basis of it will be enlarged to include humanity instead of mere fragments of it. We have seen that national honor consists in a series of potentially dramatic impulses consecrated by ideal symbols and associations. Knowing the inductive steps by which national honor came to be, our psychological experts can deductively work back from a hypothetical sentiment of international honor to supply a similar series of dramatic symbols and associations for its sustenance.

To begin with we are taking over the term honor which in itself has a great deal of psychologic "good-will," and in creating the term international honor we cannot help transferring much of the sacrosanct emotional associations which attach to all other codes of honor. As we have seen, national honor acquires most of its unreasoning intensity from the word "honor" rather than from the prefix "national." This glamor is given to us gratis, as it were, in laying the basis for the new sentiment.

Our first real task, of course, is to provide the political and physical basis for the "international" part of international honor, that is some sort of working federation of the family of nations. It is for statesmen to supply the political machinery for a federation which will not take away from the separate states any more "sovereignty" than is absolutely necessary for the creation of a working world federation. Without the physical basis for a politically integrated humanity and an outward internationalism, a sentiment of internationalism would hang in the air. Some outward expression of international honor there must be to which the new sentiment can attach itself and begin to build up its emotional associative ramifications.

A definite code of international law together with a code of accepted principles of international honor gleaned from the national codes, and approved by the international parliament, will provide a definite legal machinery around which still further associations can build themselves. An international police force will help to bring into existence the "center" for our sentiment. The more numerous the concrete realities onto which the sentiment can be grafted, the more abiding will it be. An international postal system with international stamps, an international unit of exchange, an international flag, symbols and songs, all these would have an emotional value. The more frequently the man in the streets is made to come into contact with the physical machinery around which it is expected that he mold his sentiment of international honor, the more spontaneously will it arise.

After the present war the time will be ripe for the shaping of this yet nebulous idea into a comprehensive policy. And without question this task seems to belong first to America. As a matter of fact, she has already embarked on this mission. In her resolve to "make the world safe for democracy" she is consecrating her blood and treasure not to an outworn ideal of national selfishness, but to *international honor*. This is her great justification. It has not as yet been emphasized in just these terms, for the ideal always runs ahead of its conventional expression. It will be for us, with our man of great heart and great vision as America's spokesman, to give to the world this new slogan, to make real, vital, and emotionally valid by repeated utterances, and by every device of reason, imagination and art, this thing for which we are giving our lives. The time is potent with spiritual vitality and emotional glamor, which if rightly directed by statesmen throughout the world, may be made to embody itself in this international ideal. The high task is already sanctified by the sufferings, the

AN EMOTIONAL EQUIVALENT 209

sacrifices, the lives of millions of human beings. It is but for leaders to turn to account this baptism of life which is being poured upon humanity, that the new birth to a greater humanity may come into being; that this ideal of *international honor* may be born to a conscious existence.

To expedite the process by which this new irresistible slogan may come to be adopted in the hearts of men, the idea of "advertising" seems out of place. And yet if we wish to be practical, if we wish to obtain results, we must recognize the wisdom of "efficiency" as applied to the task of popularizing an ideal yet new, just as we recognize it in our efforts to place a new article on the market. As I have said before we must take advantage of our knowledge of mass psychology. Advertising seems a crude word and yet it was by this means albeit unconscious, that our present national honor sentiment became an irresistible slogan against which reason stands helpless. So it is for us to engage after the war in a mammoth advertising campaign to put before the people of the world the commodity of *international honor,* to utilize every psychological device to appeal to the sentiments, and to create inseparable ramifying emotional associations around the ideal.

The possibilities for starting this ball of a rational sentiment along a path in which it will be able to attract to itself emotional accretions, are fertile and varied. The public school has its opportunity to present to impressionable minds the pictures of heroes of the present war with some accompanying recognition of their heroism not in defense of some country, but in defense of international honor. To the artist who paints the battlefield of the Marne, there is presented another channel, for did not INTERNATIONAL HONOR struggle for justification on that ground? The interpretative privilege of the historian should here be enlisted for the cause. A museum of INTERNATIONAL HONOR, or a hall of INTERNATIONAL HONOR wherein would be placed figures of those men who have given their services or their lives for things greater than national honor, would serve a valuable purpose here. Drama and moving pictures could strike new emotional chords in response to this appeal of enlightened honor. Here would we beg the genius of the magic pageant maker, Percy Mackaye, for aid in the creation of a thing greater than community spirit, the international spirit. What healing of the nations we might hope for if art, music, drama and literature combined to work for this end, that the new sentiment might be imbued with dramatic and emotional associations, with the emotional imperatives which, as I have shown,

AN EMOTIONAL EQUIVALENT 211

inhere in human nature and have hitherto found in national honor alone, consummate expression. By emotional appeals only will the "INTERNATIONAL HEART" grow into being upon which international honor will rest as upon the rock of Gibraltar; for it is the heart, not the mind, whence all honor impulses flow.

THE following pages contain advertisements of a few of the Macmillan books on kindred subjects

The Foreign Policy of Woodrow Wilson---1913-1917

By Edgar E. Robinson and Victor J. West

$1.75

"One of the best books on such a subject that has recently come to hand . . . a truthful presentation of one of the greatest eras the United States has ever realized . . . carries with it the intense interest that one would expect of such a book.—*The New York Evening Mail*.

The authors have recognized that there has been a great deal of unmerited criticism directed towards President Wilson for his handling of the diplomatic crises in which the United States has been involved. They believe that this criticism is due to a lack of real knowledge, not only of facts but of the farseeing and consistent policy which President Wilson has pursued since 1913.

No attempt has been made to write a history of the diplomacy of the period or to discuss with any thought of finality the multitude of questions that fill it. The paramount problems, the fundamental principles, the great decisions,—these only have been given extended treatment.

Added value is given the book by the inclusion of the President's addresses and proclamations.

THE MACMILLAN COMPANY
Publishers   64–66 Fifth Avenue   New York

America Among the Nations

By H. H. Powers,
Author of "The Things Men Fight For," etc.

Cloth, 12mo, $1.50

To arrive at an estimate of national character from the homely facts of our national history, is the purpose of this volume, as expressed by the author. He would, too, discard the time-honored prepossessions and epithets which have too long done duty with us as estimates of foreign nations, and arrive at a juster conclusion based on their actions. In short, he says, this book is an attempt at an historic interpretation of our national character and of our relation to other nations. With this purpose in mind he devotes the first part of his text to a consideration of America at home, taking up such topics as, The First Americans; The Logic of Isolation; The Great Expansion; The Break with Tradition; The Aftermath of Panama; Pan-Americanism and The Dependence of the Tropics. The second division is entitled America Among the World Powers, and considers among other things: The Greater Powers; The Mongolian Menace; Greater Japan; Germany, The Storm Center; The Greatest Empire; and The Greatest Fellowship.

THE MACMILLAN COMPANY
Publishers   64–66 Fifth Avenue   New York

Where Do You Stand?

AN APPEAL TO AMERICANS OF GERMAN ORIGIN

By HERMANN HAGEDORN,
Author of "You Are the Hope of the World," etc.

Boards, 12mo.

This is a fervent appeal to German-Americans to come out squarely and enthusiastically in support of the United States against Germany. Mr. Hagedorn thinks that the question which he makes the title of his book is a fair question for Americans to ask and he urges that it is not enough for German-Americans merely to be loyal to the United States; they must make their loyalty whole-hearted and enthusiastic. Mr. Hagedorn reviews the course of German-American opinion in this country and marshals the attitude of the typical German-American who felt that this country was pro-British and unfair to Germany, against the attitude of the typical American who felt that the German-American was unreservedly taking the German and not the American point of view. Further, Mr. Hagedorn condemns intellectual leaders among the German-Americans because they have "sulked in their tents" and have left the expression of German-American opinion to irresponsible newspapers and propagandists.

THE MACMILLAN COMPANY
Publishers   64–66 Fifth Avenue   New York

The World War and the Road to Peace

By T. B. McLeod

With an Introduction by Dr. S. Parkes Cadman.

Boards, 12mo.

This volume contains a judicial consideration of the pacifist positions and some sound advice to the men holding them. Many of the supporters of pacifism Dr. McLeod treats in short order, but he discusses at considerable length and with sympathy what may be called the humanitarian basis for the pacifist. One of the marked features of the volume is the clearness with which the author shows that Americans are all essentially pacifists —they hate war and are afraid of it, but they are undertaking this war because as Americans they feel that all that this country believes in is threatened by German aggression.

THE MACMILLAN COMPANY
Publishers   64–66 Fifth Avenue   New York